2A
Fourth Edition
Generations

SLE
SPEAKING · LISTENING · EXPRESSION

PAGODA Books

Copyright © 2012, 2008, 2001, 1997 PAGODA Academy, Inc.

All rights reserved. No part of this publication may be reproduced, stored in a retrieval system, or transmitted, in any form, or by any means, electronic, mechanical, photocopying, recording or otherwise, without the prior written permission of the copyright holder and the publisher.

Published by Wit & Wisdom
Wit & Wisdom is the professional language publishing company of the
PAGODA Education Group.
19F, PAGODA Tower, 419, Gangnam-daero,
Seocho-gu, Seoul, 06614, Rep. of KOREA
www.pagodabook.com

Imprint | PAGODA Books

First published 2012
Fourteenth impression 2022
Printed in the Republic of Korea

ISBN 978-89-6281-453-8 (13740)

Publisher	Kyung-Sil Park
Writers	Judson Wright, Jaime Dugan
Contributors	Lee Robinson, Wade Chilcoat, Patrick Farrell, Kat Paterson
Editor	Paul Adams
Advisor	Ruda Go
Illustrator	Dae Ho Kim

Acknowledgements
Simon Cosgriff, Sang Hee Kang, Song Rim Park, Hana Sakuragi, Stephen Willetts, Ian Windsor, and Gemma Young for their support
Patrick Farrell, Paul Hershberger, Phil Robinson, Tiara Smith, David Speigle, and Meredith Watson for trialing and feedback
Rich Debourke, Jay Hilalen, Jess Kroll, Gina Oh, Tiara Smith, Stephen Willetts, and Gemma Young for voice recording.

A defective book may be exchanged at the store where you purchased it.

To Our Students

The SLE program is a conversation program for adult and young adult students who want to improve their English in an enjoyable, effective, and authentic way. The book allows students to use English in a variety of contexts with an emphasis on different useful functions. Our goal is to improve your confidence in your speaking, listening, reading, and writing ability while improving your vocabulary and grammar skills. We will help you to understand not only the "How" but the "Why" of English usage.

The SLE Level 2 textbook series is meant for students with a very good understanding of the basics of English. The material in this book focuses on building students' ability to perform basic functions and use essential structures.

Contents SLE 2A

To Our Students | 3
Format of the Book | 6
Goals for the Course | 7
Meet the Thompson Family | 8

UNIT 1
Getting To Know You
Social Skills at Work and Play
☐ 11

LESSON 1 | 12
LESSON 2 | 16

UNIT 2
Talk is Cheap
Communication
☐ 27

LESSON 1 | 28
LESSON 2 | 34

UNIT 3
To Every Season
Choices and Consequences
☐ 43

LESSON 1 | 44
LESSON 2 | 50

UNIT 4
Struggles
Personal and Social Adversity
☐ 59

LESSON 1 | 60
LESSON 2 | 68

UNIT 5
There and Back Again
Travel and Transportation
☐ 77

LESSON 1 | 78
LESSON 2 | 86

Listening Dialogues | 168
Glossary | 176

UNIT 6
A Day in the Life
Day to Day Activities
☐ **95**

LESSON 1 | 96
LESSON 2 | 102

UNIT 7
It Takes All Kinds
Personalities and Habits
☐ **113**

LESSON 1 | 114
LESSON 2 | 120

UNIT 8
Good Times
Holidays and Celebrations
☐ **129**

LESSON 1 | 130
LESSON 2 | 134

UNIT 9
Picture of Health
Wellbeing
☐ **143**

LESSON 1 | 144
LESSON 2 | 148

UNIT 10
Looking Back
Bringing It All Together
☐ **157**

LESSON 1 | 158

Format of the Book:

Overall Format >
There are ten units in this textbook, each with its own focus. In each unit there are two individual lessons. The focus of the lesson is either grammatical or topical. Each unit consists of the following elements:

Warm Up >
The warm up for each lesson has its own purpose. The lesson one warm up is used as an opportunity to start thinking about the topic and includes functional language such as idioms, collocations, and tongue twisters that relate to the topic as a whole. The lesson two warm up is used as a quick review of the language used in the first lesson and a bridge to the second lesson.

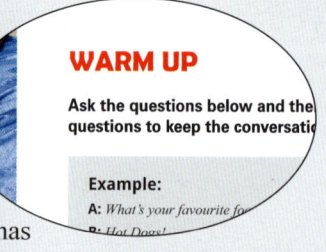

Listening >
Each listening follows the story of the Thompson family and relates to the unit topic and language points used in that unit. Each listening requires the student to make predictions based on illustrations and use communicative language to discuss what they have heard.

Language Point >
Language points occur at the start of any activity where a specific grammar or function point is used in that activity and needs to be explained to the student.

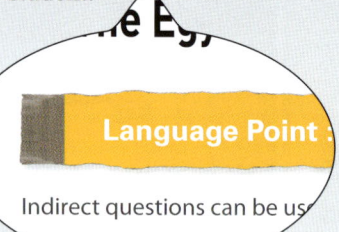

Activities >
Each lesson consists of a structured activity, a communicative activity, and a task based activity. All units include a "Bonus activity" that can add to the lesson.

Discussion Questions >
Each lesson has a short series of discussion questions that relate to the topic and encourage the use of asking follow up questions.

Boxes >
Several boxes are found throughout the text and have different functions:

- **Recycle Box**
Reminds students of language points they have used previously in SLE.

- **Third Wheel**
Gives a suggestion of how students can perform an activity with an extra student.

- **Do You Know?**
Explains the reason why language is used in a specific way.

- **Do You Remember?**
Reminds students of vocabulary from a previous lesson.

- **Tip**
Gives a tip on how students can acquire the language easier.

Segue Activity >
The segue activity consists of a reading that relates to the topic of the listening, discussion questions which check the comprehension of the reading, and a short writing task on the topic.

Goals for the Course:

1 You should be able to use the following grammatical structures:

- **a** Indirect questions
- **b** Tag questions
- **c** Comparatives and superlatives
- **d** Cause and effect using because and since
- **e** Conditionals (likely and unlikely possibilities)
- **f** Active vs. passive voice
- **g** Causative passive voice
- **h** Present perfect progressive
- **i** Reflexive pronouns

2 You should be able to perform the following functions:

- **a** Understanding when to use formal vs. informal greetings
- **b** Describing job fields and qualifications
- **c** Making suggestions and demands
- **d** Giving and receiving advice
- **e** Describing feelings and emotions
- **f** Making decisions
- **g** Describing personalities
- **h** Talking about actions happening around the same time
- **i** Discussing health problems

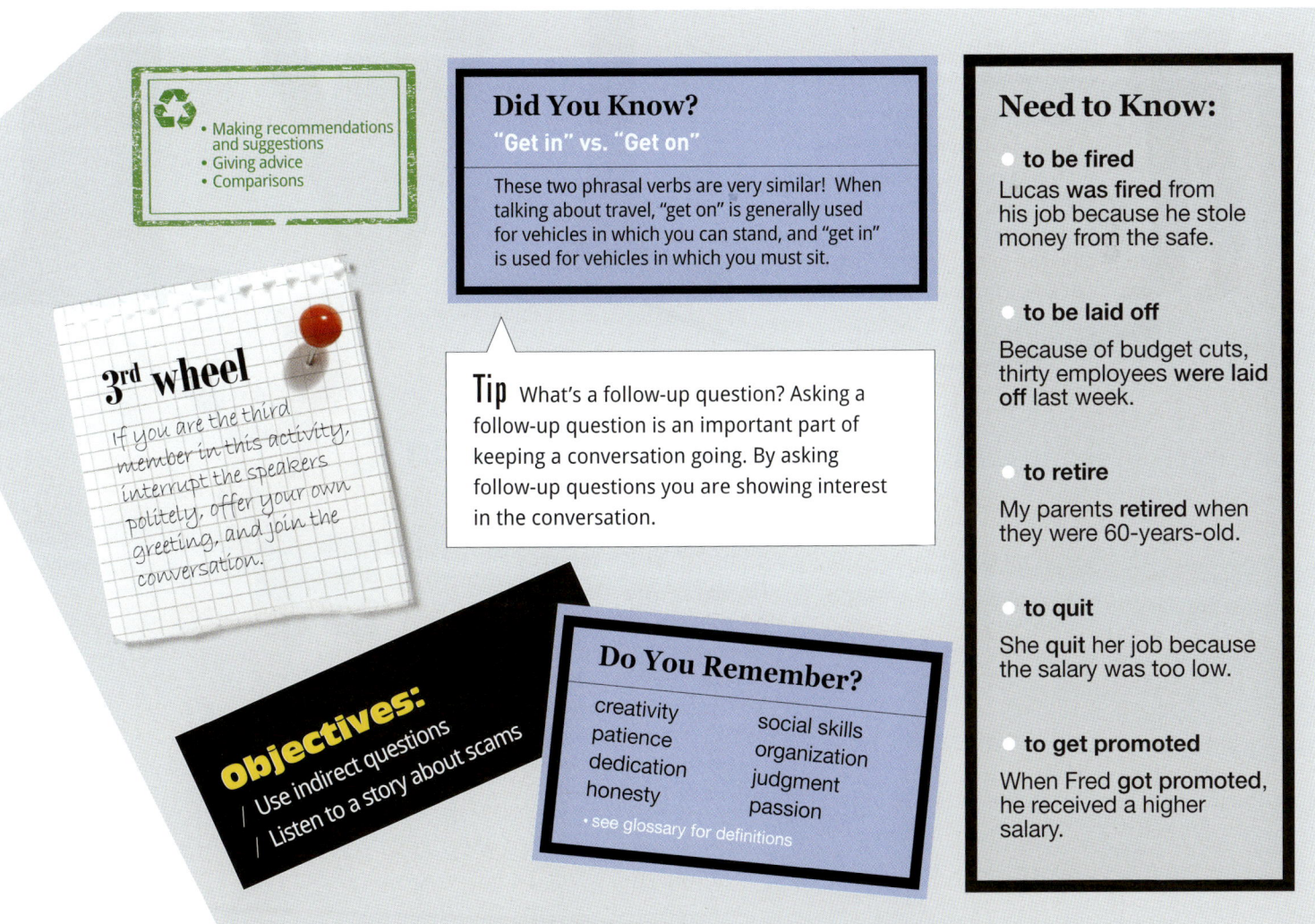

- Making recommendations and suggestions
- Giving advice
- Comparisons

Did You Know?
"Get in" vs. "Get on"

These two phrasal verbs are very similar! When talking about travel, "get on" is generally used for vehicles in which you can stand, and "get in" is used for vehicles in which you must sit.

Need to Know:

- **to be fired**
  Lucas **was fired** from his job because he stole money from the safe.

- **to be laid off**
  Because of budget cuts, thirty employees **were laid off** last week.

- **to retire**
  My parents **retired** when they were 60-years-old.

- **to quit**
  She **quit** her job because the salary was too low.

- **to get promoted**
  When Fred **got promoted**, he received a higher salary.

3rd wheel
If you are the third member in this activity, interrupt the speakers politely, offer your own greeting, and join the conversation.

Tip What's a follow-up question? Asking a follow-up question is an important part of keeping a conversation going. By asking follow-up questions you are showing interest in the conversation.

objectives:
- Use indirect questions
- Listen to a story about scams

Do You Remember?
creativity, patience, dedication, honesty, social skills, organization, judgment, passion

* see glossary for definitions

Meet the Thompson Family
Several of the activities will follow their lives and daily routines.

Jack Thompson

Age: 22
Blood type: A
Job: Senior at University

Jack is a friendly, relaxed young man, though many people think he is very lazy. He enjoys drinking with his friends and listening to his favorite band: the Crimson Kings. He will graduate from university soon and is starting to look for a new job. But not very hard.

Susan Thompson

Age: 42
Blood type: B
Job: Owns a small catering business

Susan is a logical, smart, and independent woman. She loves reading non-fiction, especially biographies. In her free time, Susan enjoys relaxing with an old movie and a large cup of tea. She recently found out that she is pregnant with her third child!

Charles Thompson

Age: 67
Blood type: O
Job: Retired

Richard's Father. Charles is an adventurous old man with the heart of a child. He doesn't always consider the consequences of his actions. When he was younger, he joined the military and traveled the world. He enjoys hiking and fishing.

Richard Thompson

Age: 65
Blood type: A
Job: Retired

Richard's Mother. Martha is a kind and quirky old woman, though sometimes she is a little forgetful. She writes poetry and secretly loves watching reality television. She is very concerned about eating healthy food.

Martha Thompson

Mr. Squiggles

Age: 3
Job: Cat

Mr. Squiggles is the playful family cat. He enjoys eating, scratching furniture, taking naps in Lisa's lap, and chasing Jack around the house. Sometimes, he likes to take Susan's things and hide them under the couch.

Age: 45
Blood type: A
Job: Marketing

Richard is a motivated, hard-working, and creative man. He enjoys spending time with his family. He is an excellent cook. He also reads lots of different newspapers. He is very good at his job, and he recently received a new promotion.

Age: 19
Blood type: AB
Job: Freshman at University

Lisa is an ambitious and outgoing young woman, though her ambition sometimes means she gets easily stressed. She graduated high school last year, and this is her first year of university. She loves going to the park on sunny days and shopping on rainy days.

Lisa Thompson

Humm... Are You Ready To Meet Them?

01 Getting To Know You
Social Skills at Work and Play

Objectives:
/ Get to know each other
/ Listen to a misunderstanding at work

WARM UP

Ask the questions below and then ask two follow-up questions to keep the conversation going!

> **Example:**
> **A:** *What's your favourite food?*
> **B:** *Hot dogs!*
> **A:** *Really? Where's the best place to get a hot dog in this city?*
> **B:** *Well... I think it's Hot Diggity Dog......*

Tip What's a follow-up question? Asking a follow-up question is an important part of keeping a conversation going. By asking follow-up questions you are showing interest in the conversation.

1 What is your favorite hobby?
  ▶ Where do you _____?
  ▶ _____?

2 What was the last movie you watched?
   Did you _____?
  ▶ _____?

3 Do you have any pets?
  ▶ _____?
  ▶ _____?

4 Have you ever lived in another country or traveled abroad?
  ▶ _____?
  ▶ _____?

5 Can you speak any foreign languages besides English?
  ▶ _____?
  ▶ _____?

LESSON 1

A. Have You Ever...?

PART 1 • Follow these instructions:

1. Hold up ten fingers.
2. Go through each item on the list below. If you **have** done the action, drop a finger.
3. Discuss some of the things you have done and ask follow-up questions.

Have you ever...

... **skipped** a class in school?
... smoked a cigarette?
... fallen asleep in a movie theatre?
... lied to your parents?
... kissed someone on the first date?
... been bungee jumping?
... dated someone older than you?
... traveled to another country alone?
... cheated on an exam?
... been **engaged**/married?

PART 2 • Ask and answer your own questions using the present perfect.

Have you ever... ... ...?

1. skied in _____?
2. _____?
3. _____?
4. _____?
5. _____?
6. _____?

Do You Remember The Present Perfect?

subject + have/has + past participle

Example:
I **have seen** that movie already.
She **has** never **been** to Hawaii.

skip school *(idiom)*: to not go to school without permission
engaged *(adj.)*: promised to marry

B. First Day of Work

> **Tip** A prediction is a guess about what you think is going to happen. Making predictions is important because it can help you to understand the listening better.

Pre-listening

Part 1 ● Have you ever been confused for somebody else? Have you ever **mistaken** a stranger for someone you thought you knew? What happened? If this has never happened to you, how do you think you would feel?

Part 2 ● Now look at the picture below. Make predictions about what happened to Richard on his first day of work. What do you think happened to Richard?

Listening TRACK 2-3

Listen to the dialogue to find out what really happened. Do you think the people are speaking formally or informally with each other?

Post-listening

Part 1 ● Discuss what happened in the dialogue. What mistake did Richard make? Was it much different from your original prediction? What happened differently?

Part 2 ● Everybody makes mistakes. What would you do in the following situations?

1. You were very sleepy in the morning. You arrive at work or class and realize that you still have your pajamas on. *I would...*

2. You wrote a very romantic email to the person you are interested in, but instead of sending it to him/her, you accidentally sent it to everyone in your class or office. *I would...*

3. You have to give an important speech in ten minutes. While you are preparing, you accidentally spill coffee all over the front of your clothes. You do not have time to go home and change. *I would...*

mistake (v.): to accidentally think someone is another person

C. You're Fired!

Talk about the following situations. What do you think is going to happen to the employee? What would you do if it were your decision?

> **Example:** During business meetings with the CEO, Grace was checking her email and sending text messages on her new smart phone.
> **A:** The CEO is probably going to *fire* her. What would you do if you were the boss?
> **B:** I would *fire* her because it's really rude to check your phone during meetings.

1 Bill did not show up to work on Thursday. He said that his grandmother had died. The problem is that he already used that excuse once before.

4 Marge has been with the company for over forty years and is finally thinking about what to do with the rest of her life.

6 Penny is the boss's daughter. She was hired and immediately given a position as a project leader. Within the first two weeks, seven workers made *complaints* about her.

Need to Know:

- **to be fired**
Lucas **was fired** from his job because he stole money from the safe.

- **to be laid off**
Because of budget cuts, thirty employees **were laid off** last week.

- **to retire**
My parents **retired** when they were sixty years old.

- **to quit**
She **quit** her job because the salary was too low.

- **to get promoted**
When Fred **got promoted**, he received a higher salary.

- **to get demoted**
The head director **got demoted** for poor performance in his department.

2 Sue *proposed* a new *budget* for the company which saved them $3.4 million dollars.

3 Pete came into his office early and caught his boss looking through his coworker's personal email.

5 Rodrigo has worked very hard at his new job. Even though most of his coworkers do less work, they have been at the company for a long time. Due to the recent economy, the company is not making enough money.

7 Todd and Mindy have been in a relationship for over a month even though it is against company policy for coworkers to date. Todd is Mindy's manager. Someone recently overheard them kissing in the stairwell and is threatening to tell their boss about the relationship.

propose *(v.)*: to make a suggestion
budget *(n.)*: a plan for spending money
complaint *(n.)*: a reason for not being satisfied

Discussion Questions

1. What are some good conversation questions to ask someone you have just met?

2. Do you get nervous when meeting new people?
   ▶ What experiences have you had that felt embarrassing or uncomfortable?

3. What do you think are some good places to meet people?
   ▶ Why do people like to go to these places to socialize?

4. What do you usually talk about with your friends?
   ▶ How about your family or your coworkers?

5. Do you think **first impressions** are important? Why or why not?
   ▶ What are the first things you notice about a person you have just met?

6. What are the qualities of a good friend?
   ▶ Why do you think so?

7. When people meet new *acquaintances*, they often talk about the weather or what they do for work. What topics do you think are safe or unsafe to talk about with people you don't know very well?

first impression *(n.)*: the sense you give someone of yourself upon first meeting
acquaintance *(n.)*: a person you know

Unit 1 Getting to Know You | 15

LESSON 2

>> WARM UP

Look at the pictures and answer the following questions for each:

> What is this person's job?
> What are the job requirements?
> Do you think he/she makes good money? What benefits does he/she enjoy?
> Which job do you think is the best? Would you like to have this job? Why or why not?

Remember to ask follow-ups!

Objectives:
/ Talk about job requirements
/ Use Informal vs. Formal greetings

A. What It Takes

Discuss the kinds of jobs available in each field below. Think of at least two examples for each. Discuss the characteristics they require for success.

Example:
I think a writer needs creativity and determination to do her job. How about you?

Do You Remember?

creativity	social skills
patience	organization
dedication	judgment
honesty	passion

• see glossary for definitions, pg.176

B. Job Interviews

Imagine that you are interviewing applicants for a job at your company. Decide what kind of company it is. Then look at each of the numbered items below. Do you think they are important qualities for a candidate? Why or why not?

> **Example:**
> **A:** *How important is it that Darren has good hair?*
> **B:** *Well, it's very important if he plans to apply for a management job. What do you think?*

1 Attitude/Self Confidence

2 Appearance
- Hair
- Speaking Ability
- Height
- Weight
- Clothing

Résumé

Name : Darren Deeds

3 *Educational background:*
Bachelor's degree in Economics from the William County College;

Master's degree in Business Administration from Princeton University

GPA: 3.2

4 *Experience:*
Five Years tutoring at A-1 Academy

5 *Personal Information:*
Age:25

Parents: Married 37 years

Blood Type: A

Religion: Roman Catholic

Hobbies: Working out, Playing the guitar, Reading mystery novels

6 *References:*
Economics professor; Former boss

Need to Know

- **degree**
  - Bachelor of Arts (BA)
  - Master of Arts (MA)
  - Doctor of Philosophy (Ph.D.)

- **undergraduate** *(adj.)*

  When I was an **undergraduate** student, I majored in English Literature.

- **graduate** *(adj.)*

  His **graduate** program took three years to complete.

---

reference *(n.)*: a person who can give information about another's ability

C. Good Morning, Sir

Language Point : Formal vs. Informal Greetings
There are different ways of greeting people, depending on the situation.

Example: Formal: *Hello, how are you?*
Informal: *Hey, what's up?*

Formal

A Good morning, sir. How are you?
B I'm doing well, thank you. How are you, Michael?
A I'm fine, thank you.

A Hello Professor Jones, how are you?
B Hi Tom, I'm doing all right, thanks. How about yourself?
A I'm doing well, thanks.

A Hi honey, did you have a good day at school?
B Hi Mom. Yeah, it was OK, I guess.
A Just OK?

Informal

A Hey Sheila, what's up? Want to go see a movie later?
B Yeah, sure! What movie do you want to see?
A Let's go see that new Brad Pitt movie.

Act out the following situations. Greet each other using an informal or formal expression depending on the situation. If the role has (Start) in it you should greet the other person first.

> **Example:**
> **A:** *Good afternoon, miss. How are you today?*
> **B:** *Very well, thank you. What may I help you with?*
> **C:** *Pardon me for interrupting. I just wanted to say thank you for the card.*

STUDENT A

3rd wheel
If you are the third member in this activity, interrupt the speakers politely, offer your own greeting, and join the conversation.

1
Role: You are a university student (Start).
Situation: You have a question about an **upcoming** exam. As you are walking on campus, you see your professor. Greet him and ask the question. Be sure to finish the conversation appropriately.

2
Role: You are a university student.
Situation: You have an important English Literature exam tomorrow morning. Another student missed a class and wants to speak to you. Greet him/her, answer the question(s), and finish the conversation appropriately.

3
Role: You are a Mom/Dad (Start).
Situation: You are **picking up** your son/daughter from middle school at the end of the day. Greet him/her, ask questions about the school day, and finish the conversation appropriately.

4
Role: You are a friend.
Situation: You made plans with a friend to go see a movie. Greet your friend, talk about which movie you want to see, and finish the conversation appropriately.

5
Role: You are a teacher (Start).
Situation: You are meeting with one of your students' parents because the student created a problem in class. Greet the parent, explain the situation, and finish the conversation appropriately.

6
Role: You are a CEO.
Situation: While you are sitting in your office, a new employee stops by to say hello. Greet him/her, ask a few questions, answer his/her questions, and finish the conversation appropriately.

upcoming *(adj.)*: happening soon
to pick up *(phrasal v.)*: to collect someone or something from a location

STUDENT B

1

Role: You are a university professor.

Situation: While you are walking on campus, one of your students approaches you. Greet him/her and answer the question. Be sure to finish the conversation appropriately.

2

Role: You are a university student (Start).

Situation: You missed your English Literature class this morning. There will be an important exam tomorrow. Greet another student that is in your class, and ask if you can see his/her notes. Finish the conversation appropriately.

3

Role: You are a son/daughter.

Situation: It is the end of the school day and your mother/father has arrived to take you home. Greet him/her, answer the questions, and finish the conversation appropriately.

4

Role: You are a friend (Start).

Situation: You made plans to go see a movie with your friend. Greet him/her, talk about which movie you want to see, and finish the conversation appropriately.

5

Role: You are a parent.

Situation: Your child's teacher wants to meet with you about a problem your child is having in school. Greet him/her, discuss the problem, and conclude the conversation appropriately.

6

Role: You are a company employee (Start).

Situation: It is your first day on the job. As you are walking to your desk, you see your boss in his/her office. Greet the CEO, introduce yourself, answer his/her questions, and finish the conversation appropriately.

Discussion Questions

1 What is your dream job?
- ▶ Why do you think this job would be good for you?

2 When considering a job, what are you most concerned about: job satisfaction or **job security**?
- ▶ Why?

3 Do you think men and women are treated equally in the workplace?
- ▶ Why or why not?

4 Do you think it is fair that employers prefer to hire graduates from **prestigious** universities?
- ▶ Why or why not?

5 If you started your own company, what kind of company would it be?
- ▶ Why?

6 After graduating from university, how important is it to get a job related to your major?
- ▶ Why do you think so?

7 What will you do if you cannot find the job that you want after you graduate?
- ▶ Why will you do this?

8 What is the most boring job in the world?
- ▶ How about the most interesting job? Why do you think so?
- ▶ How about the most dangerous job? Why do you think so?

UNIT 1 REVIEW

How well can you use:
- ☐ Present perfect review: **subject + have/has + past participle**?
- ☐ Formal vs. Informal greetings?
- ☐ Job skills and attributes?

What do you need to study more?

job security *(n.)*: the knowledge that an employee will not lose his or her job
prestigious *(adj.)*: having a good reputation

Activity: Downsizing

You and your classmates are supervisors at a company. The CEO has decided to make the company smaller. One of your workers has to be laid off. The qualifications of each worker are listed below. Decide which of these individuals should be let go. After you are finished, discuss your choice with others in the class.

Name	Christie	Roger	Melissa	Don
Age	34	27	21	47
Marital Status	Divorced	Single	Engaged	Married
Dependents	2 children	Mother	None	Wife and 18-year-old son
Education	Vocational high school graduate	High school dropout	College student	Graduate school at night
Health	Used to be an alcoholic; **sober** for 7 years	**Disabled**, but this does not affect his work	Excellent	A little overweight
Seniority	8 years	5 years	2 years	6 years
Other qualities	Slow worker / gets along well with everyone / sometimes late / a little moody but honest	Good worker / good relationship with coworkers / sometimes late / friendly	Average worker / liked by most coworkers / frequently late / friendly and outgoing	Efficient worker / does not get along well with others / never late / quiet and often **grouchy**
Future	Would like to keep her current position	Hopes to get a promotion in this company	Her uncle is the company CEO	Will probably change jobs when he finishes school

1. Who would your first choice be? Why?
2. Who would your second choice be? Why?
3. Who do you think deserves to keep their job? Why?

sober *(adj.)*: not influenced by alcohol
disabled *(adj.)*: a physical or mental condition that limits a person's ability
grouchy *(adj.)*: having a bad temper or being in a bad mood

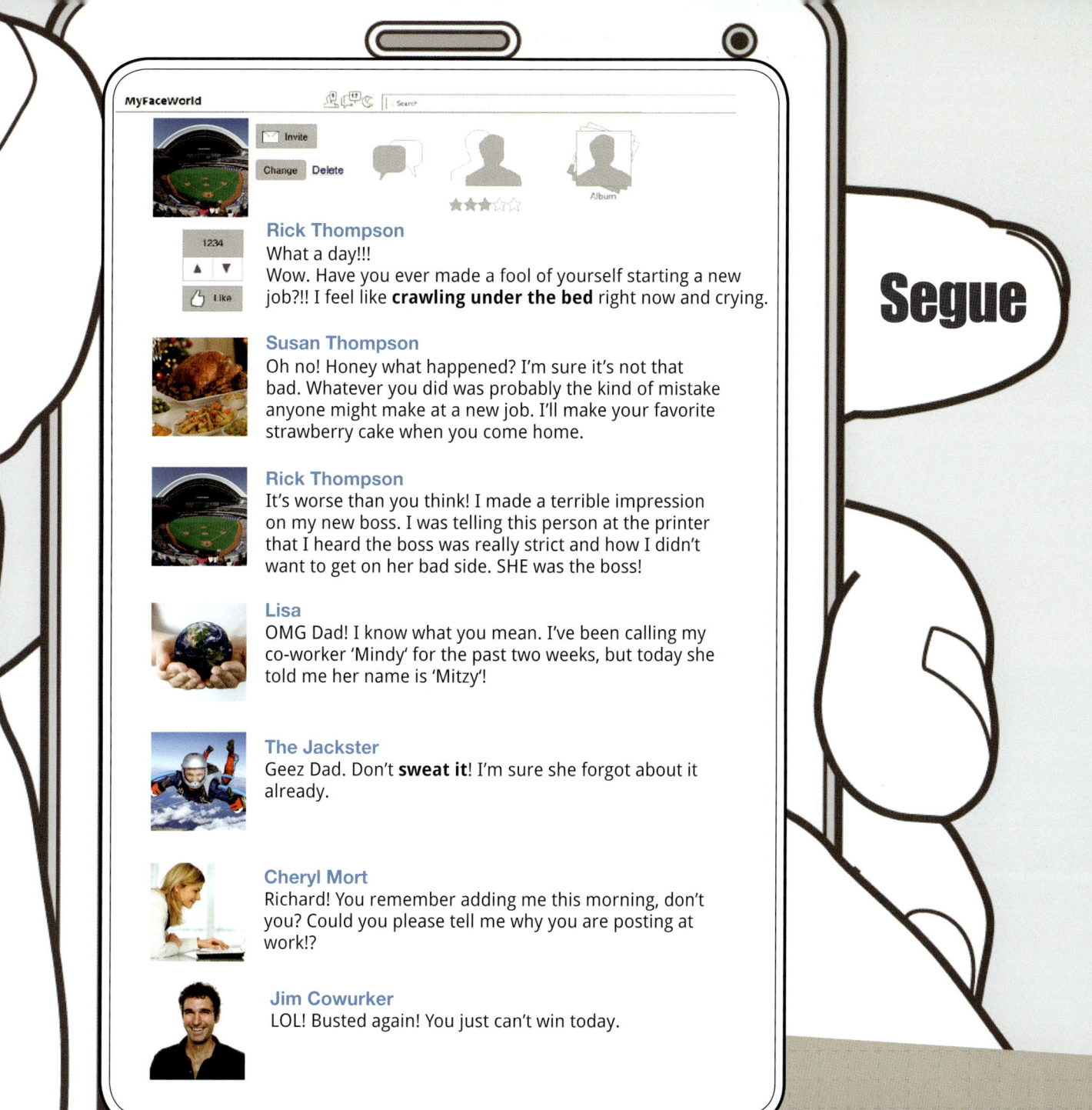

A. Discussion
1. Do you communicate with your friends and family using social network sites? Why or why not?
2. Richard says that he **"feels like crawling under the bed."** Have you ever been in a situation where you felt like crawling under the bed? What happened?
3. Jack tells Richard not to **"Sweat it"** or worry. Do you think Richard is overreacting to the situation?

B. Writing
Write a short response of 4-6 sentences to Richard telling him about a time you were in a similar situation, or try to make him feel better about his situation.

Unit 1 Getting to Know You | 25

02
Talk is Cheap
Communication

Objectives:
/ Use indirect questions
/ Listen to a story about scams

WARM UP

PART 1

Do you think it is polite to ask the following questions to someone you have just met? Why or why not?

- How old are you?
- Are you married?
- Where do you work?
- What kind of car do you drive?
- What is your religion?
- What's your blood type?
- Do you have children?
- Where did you buy that dress?
- What university did you go to?
- Do you come here often?

COLLOCATIONS

- **say a word**
  He didn't *say a word* about my new haircut.
- **strictly speaking**
  Strictly speaking, a tomato is a fruit and not a vegetable because it has seeds.
- **get the message across**
  His loud voice and serious tone really *got the message across*.
- **conflicting information**
  We're receiving *conflicting information* about who won the race.

IDIOMS

- **loud and clear**
  You don't need to repeat yourself; I got your message *loud and clear*.
- **speak your mind**
  I'm so angry at her! I'm going to call her right now and *speak my mind* about the situation.
- **pour your heart out**
  When we went out to dinner last night, Jim *poured his heart out* about the divorce.
- **My lips are sealed.**
  Don't worry, I won't tell anyone about your money problems. *My lips are sealed*.

TONGUE TWISTER

Red leather, yellow leather. Red leather, yellow leather.
Red leather, yellow leather. Red leather, yellow leather.
Red leather, yellow leather. Red leather, yellow leather.
Red leather, yellow leather. Red leather, yellow leather.

LESSON 1

A. Do You Know...?

Language Point: Indirect Questions

Why do you think the older woman is angry at Lisa?

Indirect questions are often used to be more polite. For example, if you are talking to a stranger, an information question can sound too direct.

Example
Direct: *What time is it?*
Indirect: *Could you tell me what time it is?*

◇ Notice the word order is **not** switched like in a direct question.
Also remember:
- Yes/No questions require *if or whether.*
- The auxiliary verb *do* is not used in indirect questions.

Example
Direct question:
Does the express train stop in Springfield?
Indirect question: *Can you tell me if the express train stops in Springfield?*

main questions
Do you know
Can you tell me
Have you heard

main statements
I don't know
I can't remember
Please tell me
I was wondering

indirect question
What
Where
When
Who
Why
How
if (for yes/no)

subject + verb + object

Discuss the following:

- Identify the indirect question(s) in each dialogue and underline them.
- What is the situation? Where is it taking place?
- What do you think the relationship is between the people?

1
A: Hi there. It's Jinny, right?
B: Ya. What can I do for you?
A: I need to find out if there was any homework from our last class.
B: Oh sure. We had to read and respond to the essay on page 32.

2
A: Why did you do it?
B: I don't know what you're talking about! Can you prove I did it? Where is your **proof**?
A: Don't **play games** with me. We have **witnesses**!
B: Oh. In that case... tell me if I can call my lawyer now.

3
A: I'm almost finished with all of my homework!
B: Great! I was wondering if you will have time to help me do the laundry.
A: No way. That was my chore last week.

4
A: Reynolds! This is the third time this week. Would you like to tell me why you were late?
B: I'm so sorry, ma'am. The subway wasn't running well.
A: I don't know if I believe that. Peterson takes the same subway, and he wasn't late!

5
A: Excuse me, but could you tell me what time it is?
B: Of course. It's half past four.
A: Thanks!
B: No problem.

6
A: Do you have any idea how he did it?
B: I can't remember what he pushed. I think he pushed two buttons on the remote control at the same time.
A: Um, do you know what that **beeping** sound is?
B: Maybe we should call **tech support**.

proof *(n.)*: something that indicates truth
play games *(idiom.)*: try to gain an advantage by being dishonest
witness *(n.)*: a person who sees an action in progress
beep *(n.)*: a sound made by something electronic
tech support *(n.)*: help from people who provide assistance for computers

Unit 2 Talk is Cheap | 29

B. The Egyptian Koala

Language Point: Uses of Indirect Questions.

Indirect questions can be used to ask questions that sound more polite.

Example:
A: *Would you mind telling me **what your account number is**?*

They can also be used to clarify or confirm information.
B: *Why do you want to know **what my bank account number is**?*
A: *I want to send some money to your account.*
B: *Oh. In that case, I don't mind telling you **what my account information is**.*

Pre-listening

When it comes to getting information, who do you believe? Go through the list of information sources below.

1. Do you think this source of information is trustworthy? Why or why not?

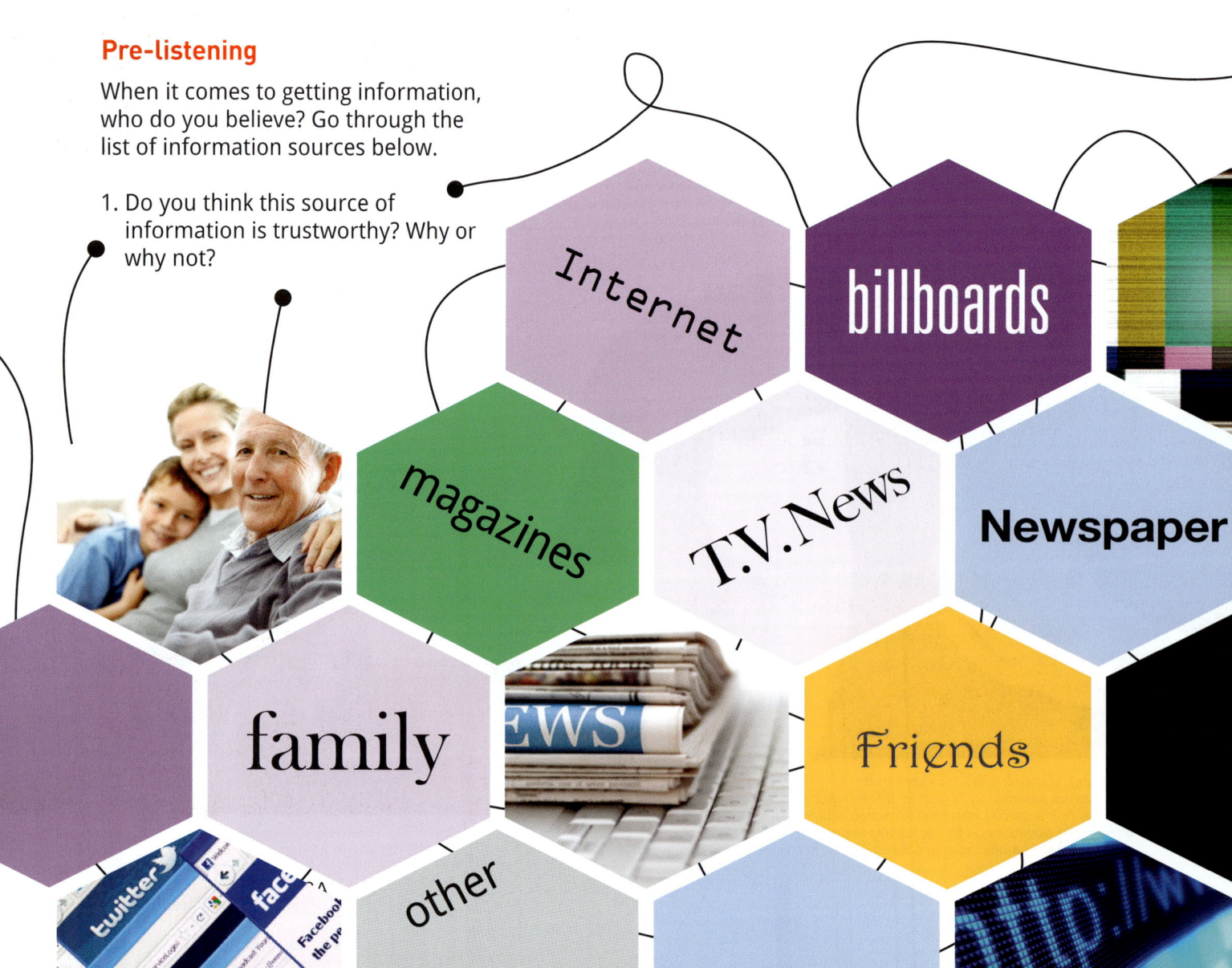

2. If two sources give conflicting information, how do you decide which is true?

Now look at the picture below. Before listening to the conversation, make predictions about what you think is happening in this situation.

Listening TRACK 4-5

Now listen to the following dialogue and see if your predictions were correct. Listen again and pay attention to the indirect questions.

Post-listening

Discuss what happened in the story. What is the problem? Have you ever experienced a situation where someone tried to **scam** you? Do you know someone who was scammed?

Do you think older people are more likely than young to believe news sources or are they more **skeptical**? Why?

---

scam *(n.)*: to trick someone to give money
skeptical *(adj.)*: having doubts about something

Unit 2 Talk is Cheap | 31

C. Have You Heard...?

Act out the following situations. Change the direct questions to indirect questions and follow up by making some of your own questions. Use the chart on pg. 28 for help.

Example: Jim's weekend plans

1. What is Jim doing this weekend?
   - **A:** *Do you know what Jim is doing this weekend?*
   - **B:** *I'm not sure. He said something about maybe going to a party.*

2. Is he going scuba diving with his friends?
   - **A:** *Did he say if he is going scuba diving with his friends?*
   - **B:** *Ah, yes. He did say something about that...*

STUDENT A

1
Is there a new movie at the cinema?
(*Do you know...*)
- a. Where is it playing?
- b. What time is it playing?
- c. Is it interesting?

2
Is there an express train going to......?
(*Could you tell me...*)
- a. Where is the closest express train station?
- b. How often does it come?
- c. How long does it take?
- d. How much does it cost?

3
What English language courses are offered at this school?
- a. Do I have to take a level test?
- b. Are the courses good?
- c. How much are the course fees?

4
What kind of cell phone do you have?
- a. What company is it made by?
- b. What kind of features does it have?
- c. Do you like it?

3rd wheel

if you are the third member of this activity, offer different information than, or agree with, student B.

STUDENT B

1
What area do you live in?
(*I was wondering...*)
- a. Is it a nice place?
- b. How long have you lived there?
- c. What is your house like?

2
Was Jack at the meeting yesterday?
(*Have you heard...*)
- a. Why didn't Jack come?
- b. Has he missed many meetings?
- c. Where is Jack now?

3
Do you have any cash?
- a. Could you lend me ten dollars?
- b. Can I borrow the money right now?
- c. When do I have to pay you back?

4
Did you see (*name of television show*) last night?
- a. What happened to the main character?
- b. What happened in the end?
- c. What do you think will happen next time?

Discussion Questions

1. When do you have to start conversations with people you do not know?
   ▶ Do you remember a situation when you had to ask a stranger for help?

2. Who is the rudest person you have met?
   ▶ What was he or she like?

3. Do you find it difficult to interrupt other people?
   ▶ Why or why not?
   ▶ Do you dislike it when other people interrupt you?

4. Why do you think people like to listen to gossip?
   ▶ Have you heard any interesting gossip recently?

5. Do you feel comfortable asking friends for favors?
   ▶ What kinds of favors have you asked friends for?

6. Are you the kind of person who takes orders well, or do you hate being told what to do?
   ▶ Why do you think you are this way?

7. What would be some polite questions to ask the following people?
   ▶ Your professor
   ▶ Your parents
   ▶ The person sitting next to you on the subway
   ▶ A classmate
   ▶ A police officer

   How about some impolite questions?

LESSON 2

>> WARM UP

Objectives:
/ Use Tag questions

What is body language?

> Why is it important for communication?
> Have you ever had to communicate with someone who could not speak your language?
> What happened?

Part 1

Pretend that you are in another country and you do not speak the native language of that country. Act out the body language that you would use when you want to say the following:

- "Where's the bathroom?"
- "I'm lost! Where is the subway station?"
- "I want a small coffee to go."
- "Help! Someone just stole my wallet!"

Part 2

What are some other questions you might have to ask in a foreign country?
Make a list:

1 _____
2 _____
3 _____

Now decide how you would communicate these questions without being able to speak the language.

A. This Is Delicious, Isn't It?

What's a Tag? A tag is something small connected to something bigger. Like a shirt tag.

Language Point : Asking Tag Questions

Speakers ask yes/no questions when they do not have previous knowledge about the topic.

Example: *Are you a vegetarian?*

Speakers generally ask tag questions when they have previous knowledge or expectations, but they want to check information or seek agreement.

Example: *You're a vegetarian,* **aren't you?**
— statement — question tag

Tip Informally it is common to replace the tag with the word "right."
You understand, right?

⊕ Positive statement
The sky is blue, → **⊖ Negative tag** isn't it?

Statement - - - - - - - - - - - - - - - - - - **Questions tag**

⊖ Negative statement
You don't like onions, → **⊕ Positive tag** do you?

Part 1

Complete each of the following questions by adding the appropriate tag.

1. You're a famous movie star, _____?
2. You have a coat, _____?
3. She's not from Canada, _____?
4. He should send his resume, _____?

Try these. They're a little bit harder.

5. He used to live in Sydney, _____?
6. Everyone came on time, _____?
7. Nobody has been to China, _____?

Language Point : Responding to Tag Questions

Positive statement + negative tag	Agreeing	Disagreeing
You **like** pizza, **don't** you?	Yes, I do.	No, I don't.
He **can** drive a car, **can't** he?	Yes, he can.	No, he can't.
They **are** alright, **aren't** they?	Yes, they are	No, they aren't.

Negative statement + positive tag	Agreeing	Disagreeing
It **isn't** cold outside, **is** it?	No, it isn't.	Yes, it is.
You **aren't** sick, **are** you?	No, I'm not.	Yes, I am.
He **isn't** married, **is** he?	No, he isn't.	Yes, he is.

◇ Note:
We sometimes add "actually" before the disagreeing statement. Actually, it is cold.

Part 2 ●

Finish the tag question then match it to the appropriate response on the right.

1. This is good coffee, _____?   a. No, he doesn't.
2. You speak English, _____?   b. No, she wasn't.
3. You can come to my party, _____?   c. Yes, it is.
4. He doesn't like to study, _____?   d. No, I can't.
5. You will help me, _____?   e. Yes, I do.
6. She was absent yesterday, _____?   f. No, I won't.

B. You Don't, Do You?

Ask and respond to tag questions by doing the following:

1 One person asks the person on his/her left a tag question using a positive or negative tag.
2 The second person should agree or disagree with the statement and give a reason why.
3 Repeat Steps 1-2 until all of the questions have been asked.

Example:

can drive
not be late
can't swim
can dance

A: *You can drive, can't you?*
B: *Yes I can. I have a driver's license. You won't be late, will you?*
C: *No, I won't. I'm always early. You can't swim, can you?*
D: *Actually, Yes I can. I learned when I was in elementary school. You can dance well, can't you?*

- shouldn't smoke
- haven't heard
- will get embarrassed
- often lie
- can't sing well
- ate too much again last night
- don't like ice cream
- won't get lost

- have never worn makeup
- enjoy gambling
- don't study hard
- don't like teachers
- don't shower often
- think Paris is beautiful
- don't think English is boring
- English is really hard

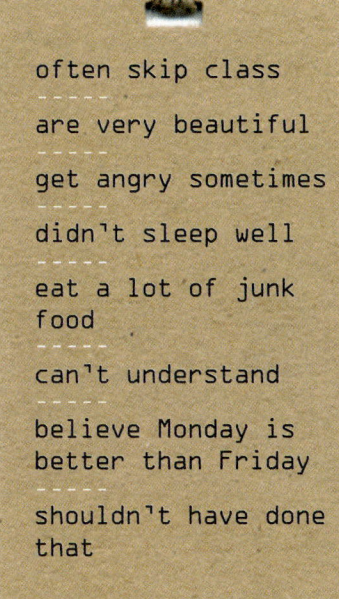

- often skip class
- are very beautiful
- get angry sometimes
- didn't sleep well
- eat a lot of junk food
- can't understand
- believe Monday is better than Friday
- shouldn't have done that

C. Tag Communication Party

Part 1 ● You are at a party with some of the Thompson's friends. Even though the guests are strangers, you have heard a little bit about each of them. Take on the roles of the various people at the party. Use tag questions to confirm or clarify information you have heard about the other people. For each question, role-play a follow-up discussion about that topic.

> **Example: Walter, Candy, and Todd**
>
> **Walter:** *So, Candy, you're a school teacher, aren't you?*
>
> **Candy:** *Yes, I am! I teach third grade Math.*
>
> **Walter:** *Do you like it?*
>
> **Candy:** *I love it. It is fun to teach children new things. Todd, you're a dance instructor, aren't you?*
>
> **Todd:** *Yes, I am!*

Part 2 ● Now make up your own character. Show your character's information to someone else and act out the situation again.

1. Your hobby _____

2. Your hometown _____

3. Something interesting about you _____

Discussion Questions

1. Are you good at **networking**?
   ▶ Do you use social network sites? Which ones?

2. Which sources of information are more **trustworthy** and accurate than others?
   ▶ Why do you think so?

3. How would life be different without the Internet and mobile phones?
   ▶ How would you communicate with your friends and family?

4. Do you prefer face-to-face communication, or do you prefer communicating through technology (e.g., Internet, mobile phone)?
   ▶ What advantages does each have?

5. When was the last time you had a **misunderstanding** with someone?
   ▶ Where were you?
   ▶ What happened?

6. How would you stay in touch with friends and family if you moved to another country?
   ▶ What problem does this kind of communication cause?

7. Is it important to learn about the culture of another country before traveling to that country?
   ▶ Why do you think so?

UNIT 2 REVIEW

How well can you use :
- ☐ Asking and responding to indirect questions?
- ☐ Asking and responding to tag questions?

What do you need to study more?

---

networking *(n.)*: getting to know other people for business purposes
trustworthy *(adj.)*: something or someone that can be believed
misunderstanding *(n.)*: a mistake made while communicating

Activity: 20 Questions

Work as a class or in small groups. One student thinks of any person, place, or thing he/she can think of (Superman, the Pyramids, ice cream, etc.). The other students take turns asking questions to find out what person, place, or thing was chosen. The questions should be of the "yes" or "no" variety. The person who chose can only respond with either "yes" or "no".

Start off with broad questions and then slowly narrow them down. You can only ask up to twenty questions.

Example:
Student A: *Is it something you eat?*
Student B: *Yes, it is.*
Student C: *Is it cold?*
Student B: *Yes.*
Student D: *It's ice cream, isn't it?*

Segue

Read the three following emails from Grandma's inbox and decide which look legitimate and which look like scams:

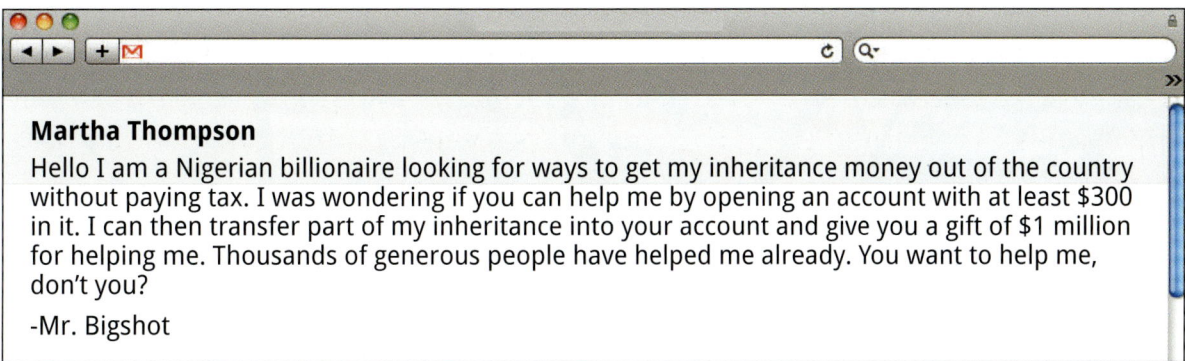

Martha Thompson

Hello I am a Nigerian billionaire looking for ways to get my inheritance money out of the country without paying tax. I was wondering if you can help me by opening an account with at least $300 in it. I can then transfer part of my inheritance into your account and give you a gift of $1 million for helping me. Thousands of generous people have helped me already. You want to help me, don't you?

-Mr. Bigshot

Mr. or Mrs. Martha Thompson

The internet is not always a safe and secure place! It is full of viruses and malware that can infect your computer. Your infected computer can be used by criminals to spam others, gain access to sensitive information, or even take over the world! By clicking on the link below you can download free software that will protect your computer.

http//:www.phishhook.com

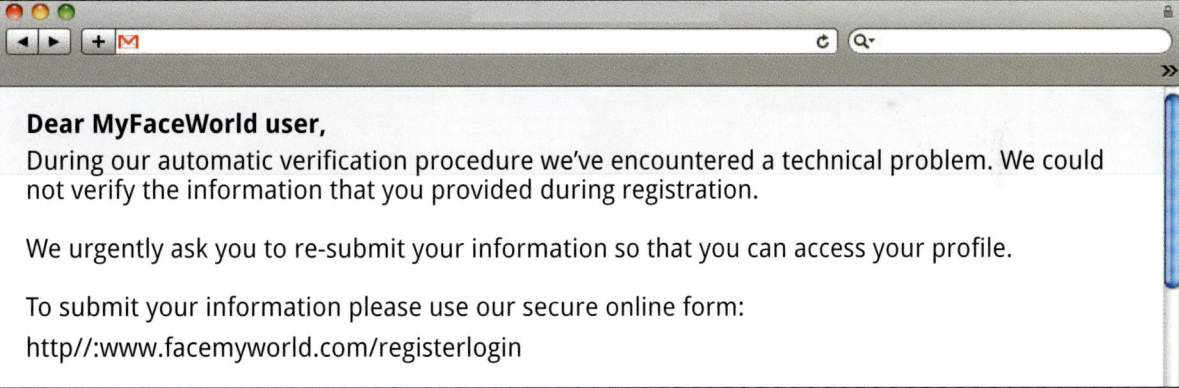

Dear MyFaceWorld user,

During our automatic verification procedure we've encountered a technical problem. We could not verify the information that you provided during registration.

We urgently ask you to re-submit your information so that you can access your profile.

To submit your information please use our secure online form:

http//:www.facemyworld.com/registerlogin

A. Discussion

1. Which emails look like **scams**? Why do you think so? Is the language used formal or informal?
2. Have you ever received scam emails? What did they promise or ask for?
3. Do you know any stories about people who were scammed by email or over the phone? What happened to them?
4. Do you think governments are doing enough to fight cybercrime? Is it possible to be safe on the internet? What can we do to protect ourselves?

B. Writing

Write your own email scam of 6-8 sentences to Grandma. Try to make the scam as believable as possible.

Your teacher can decide who he/she thinks has written the best one.

03
To Every Season
Choices and Consequences

Objectives:
/ Use comparatives and superlatives
/ Listen to a story about a bad date

WARM UP

PART 1

How is your _____ different now than it was five years ago? Why?

- Work/School
- Family
- Appearance
- Social life
- Hobby preference
- English skill

What was the best year of your life? Why do you think so?

COLLOCATIONS

- **as good as it gets**
  My new job is *as good as it gets*. I go to work whenever I want.
- **never been better**
  She said that she's *never been better* than she is right now.
- **better than ever**
  The new version of their software is *better than ever!*

IDIOMS

- **once in a lifetime**
  Meeting my idol would be a *once in a lifetime* experience.
- **open doors**
  Getting a masters degree could certainly *open a lot of doors* for you.

LESSON 1

A. Actions Speak Louder Than Words

Language Point : Comparing People, Places, and Things

Comparing two things

- Susie is **younger than** Billy.
- The new university looks much **more** modern **than** the previous one.
- Boston is **less** crowded **than** New York City.
- She is **much neater than** her sister.
- Cole is always **hungrier than** Pam.

Comparing more than two things

- Thailand is **the hottest** country I have been to.
- **The best** time to study is in the Fall.
- The bride felt like **the prettiest** woman in the world.
- Last night on T.V. I watched **the most** interesting program I have seen.
- Romantic Comedy IV is **the worst** movie of all time.

Which part of the following statements do you agree or disagree with? Give reasons for your opinion. Ask follow-up questions.

Example:
A: *English and math are easy subjects.*
B: *I think math is much harder than English.*
A: *Why?*
B: *My mother is from Canada, so English is easier for me. I have spoken English since I was very young.*

1. Japan and China are great vacation spots.
2. Watching talk shows is more interesting than watching documentaries.
3. Firefighters, police officers, and paramedics have the toughest jobs.
4. Bungee jumping and skydiving are the most dangerous hobbies.
5. Sending text messages is more convenient than speaking on the phone.
6. Buses, trains, and taxis are economical types of public transportation.
7. _____ and _____ are the most important parts of a healthy diet.
8. _____ and _____ are the worst chores.

B. Blind Dating Blues

Pre-listening

1. What are the most important considerations when preparing for a date?
   ▶ The restaurant, the food, your choice of clothing?

2. What was your best date?
   ▶ What was your worst? Why?

3. Where would you go on an ideal date?

Listening TRACK 6-7

Now look at the picture below. Considering what you just discussed, make predictions about what you think is happening on Jack's date.

Post-listening

1. Discuss what happened in the story. What is the problem?
   ▶ Are there any possible solutions?
   ▶ What would you do in Jack's situation?

2. Have you ever been on a **blind date**?
   ▶ What was it like?

blind date (n.): A date in which the two people have never met before

C. Money Makes the World Go Round

The Thompson family is making some important decisions in the near future. Each generation wants something different. Decide why they want the thing they chose and then say which one YOU would choose and why.

FAMILY CAR

REVA PACER

Richard's choice

SPECS	RATING (OUT OF 5)
Speed	🚗🚗🚗
Safety	🚗🚗🚗
Appearance	😊😊😊
Cost	$ $ $
Service Plan	🚗🚗🚗🚗🚗

46 | SLE Generations 2A

Example:

A: Lisa wants the Takuro Spirit because it is **faster** than the Reva Pacer.

B: Yes, but Richard doesn't like it because it is the **most expensive**.

C: It is a family car, so it should be safe. Charles prefers the Branson. He thinks it's **safer than** the Reva Pacer.

A: I would go with Richard's choice. The service plan is **the best**.

Takuro Spirit

Branson ZX-12

Lisa's choice

Charles's choice

Specs	Rating (Out of 5)	Specs	Rating (Out of 5)
Speed	🚗🚗🚗🚗	Speed	🚗🚗🚗🚗
Safety	🚗	Safety	🚗🚗🚗🚗🚗
Appearance	😊😊😊😊	Appearance	😊😊
Cost	$ $ $ $ $	Cost	$ $ $
Service Plan	🚗🚗🚗	Service Plan	🚗🚗🚗🚗

Housekeeper

Greta

Reginald   **Mitzy**

	Susan's choice	Martha's choice	Jack's choice
Specs	Rating (Out of 5)	Rating (Out of 5)	Rating (Out of 5)
Punctual	😊😊😊😊😊	😊😊😊	😊
Hardworking	😊😊😊😊	😊😊😊	😊😊
Efficient	😊😊	😊😊😊😊	😊😊
Cost	$ $	$ $ $ $ $	$ $ $ $
Experience	😊😊😊	😊😊😊😊😊	😊

punctual *(adj.)*: arriving on time
efficient *(adj.)*: able to produce results without wasting time

Discussion Questions

1. What is an important decision you have made?
   ▶ What was the outcome?

2. Which would you like better, staying in your home country for the rest of your life or living overseas for the rest of your life?
   ▶ What are the good and bad points of each?

3. What are some major changes in your life that have taken place in the past two years?
   ▶ How did you **handle** these transitions?

4. Many people believe that running their own business is more rewarding than working for a large company. Which do you think is better?
   ▶ What are some reasons?

5. Who do you think has a more satisfying life, people who get married or people who stay single?
   ▶ Why do you think so?

6. Some people prefer office jobs, while others prefer the kind of work that allows them to move around. Which kind of job would you prefer?

7. What's your favorite thing to do during your free time?
   ▶ Which is better, staying in for a quiet night or going out for an all-nighter?

handle *(v.)*: to deal with a difficult situation

Unit 3 To Every Season | 49

LESSON 2

>> WARM UP

Objectives:
/ Use because and since

Do you remember lesson 1? What things do you need to consider when making decisions about the following?

Example: *When buying a new car, the **most important** things for me are color and safety.*

- choosing a university
- finding a job
- finding a boyfriend/girlfriend
- buying a new computer
- choosing a vacation destination

Location	Cost	Compensation
Appearance	Safety	Adventure
Reputation	Distance	Length of Time

A. Why Did You Do That?

Language Point: Statements of Cause and Effect Using Because and Since

Clauses beginning with because and since are used to talk about the cause of something. The main clause is the effect.

Example:

A: *I am so tired today.*
B: *Why do you feel tired?*
A: *I feel tired **because I only slept for two hours last night!***

Because and *since* clauses come in either the beginning of a sentence or at the end.

Example:

*They received a high score on the exam **because** they studied hard.*
         effect   cause

Since *I start work at 8 o'clock in the morning, I leave my house at 7:30 A.M.*
         cause   effect

◇ Notice that when the cause comes first, it must be followed by a comma.

Part 1

A. Match the causes and effects.

1 Since my dad won the lottery,   a) our flight to Hawaii was cancelled.

2 I hate eating seafood   b) I asked my friend to pay for lunch.

3 Because there was a snowstorm last night,   c) because he broke his leg.

4 John quit the soccer team   d) because it makes me sick.

5 Since I left my wallet at home,   e) he spent one million dollars on a new house.

B. Finish these sentences in your own words.

1 Since it costs so much money to buy a house _____

2 Because we don't have class tomorrow _____

3 My best friend doesn't have to _____ since _____

4 _____ is my favourite food because _____

Part 2 •
Practice talking about cause and effect. Ask follow-up questions.

> **Example:** need money
>
> **A:** *Why do you need money?*
> **B:** *Because I need more money to pay for tuition, I got a part-time job.*
> **C:** *Oh yeah? What kind of work do you do?*
> **B:** *Since my major is statistics, I got a job at a market research company.*

Why do you.....

1 need to study hard?

2 have to buy a new smart phone?

3 need to get a driver's license?

4 feel tired ?

5 need to get in shape ?

6 want to travel the world?

7 want to study abroad next year?

8 need to get good grades ?

9 think about your future?

B. Would You Rather?

• Using comparative and superlative adjectives

Answer the following questions using comparative and superlative adjectives. Give a reason for your decision. Remember to ask follow-up questions.

> **Example:** ...be rich and unhappy or poor and happy?
> **A:** *Would you rather be rich and unhappy or poor and happy?*
> **B:** *I would rather be rich and unhappy because people who are rich live in bigger houses and drive nicer cars.*
> **A:** *It wouldn't bother you to be unhappy all the time?*

1 ...forget who you are or forget who everyone else is?

2 ...not be able to use your phone or not be able to brush your teeth?

3 ...have a big group of friends or one very close friend?

4 ...be 125cm tall or 240 cm tall?

5 ...always lose at games or never be able to play games?

6 ...always have to say everything on your mind or never speak again?

7 ...lose your legs or lose your arms?

8 ...find true love or win $10,000,000?

9 ...sing everything you say or dance every time you move?

10 ...have one finger which is longer than the others or ten very short fingers?

Unit 3 To Every Season | 53

C. Bringing It All Together

Practice using comparatives and cause and effect clauses to make a story about what happened in each of the four situations below.
Use the topics and pictures below to make at least four statements for each situation.

Jack and Jill

Larry

 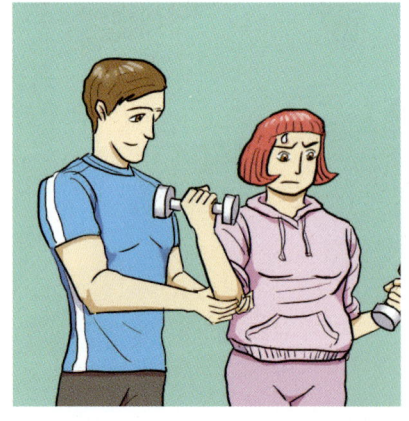 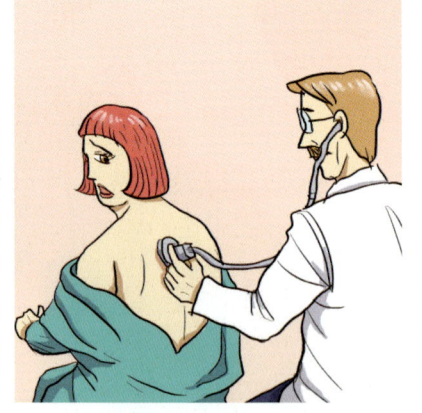 

Mary

Donald

Discussion Questions

1 What is an ideal friend like?
  ▶ Why do you think some friendships are longer than others?

2 What would your perfect home be like?
  ▶ Where would it be and how much would it cost?

3 What was the worst decision you have ever made?
  ▶ What happened because of this decision?

4 What is the best thing that could happen to you in your life right now?
  ▶ Why would you want this?

5 Where is the best place in the world to live?
  ▶ Why would you live there?

6 What are your **pet peeves**?
  ▶ Why do these things annoy you?

7 What is the best vacation you have ever had?
  ▶ Why was it so good?

8 When you are making decisions with a group of people, do you usually **go along with** what everyone else wants to do, or do you try and convince others to follow your opinion?

UNIT 3 REVIEW

How well can you use:
☐ Comparatives and Superlatives?
☐ Cause and effect with *because* and *since*?

What do you need to study more?

pet peeve *(n.)*: something that annoys a person
go along with *(phrase)*: to agree to someone's wants

Activity: Once Upon a Time

As a class, create a chain story about the Thompsons using "Because" and "Since" clauses. Topics for the story are listed below, or you can start with your own.

Topics

1. Richard embarrassed himself at work.
2. Jack ran away from his date.
3. Grandma opened an email.
4. Susan made a strawberry cake.
5. Mr. Squiggles was hungry.
6. Lisa made plans to see a movie.
7. Grandpa got sick.
8. Cousin Joe went abroad.
9. The family went on a cruise.
10. Grandpa and Lisa walked through the park.

Because Richard was rude to his boss, he bought her flowers.

Since his boss is very allergic to flowers, she started to sneeze.

Because she couldn't stop sneezing, she had to go home.

Since she left the office for the day, Richard.....

56 | SLE Generations 2A

LastDitchDating.com

This Month's Featured

Segue

Luscious and Lonely
Name: Terry Bull
Age: 24

Statement I consider myself a hopeless romantic. I like long walks on moonless nights through the woods. I enjoy talking to myself and staring contests. I want to meet someone who likes spending quiet evenings with just me and my mother. Interested? Don't send anything. Just come over, NOW.

Action Man
Name: Jim Shorts
Age: 23

Statement What are you waiting for!? I am ready to pounce! Let's work out together! All day, every day! I love running, jumping, spinning, dancing, kicking, and anything that ends in -ing. Send me a list of medals you have won and body fat percentage. I'll get back to you when I have time.

Moon Unit
Name: Estelle Hurtz
Age: 21

Statement Hi fun guy! It's me calling from outer space! When was the last time you went on a date and woke up in the hippo cage at the zoo? My last fourteen boyfriends had nervous breakdowns. If you think you are interested, send me a hair sample, a song, and a sea shell!

The Manager
Name: Barb Dwyer
Age: 22

Statement If you like working hard in a relationship and know who the boss is, we could try dating. I hate action movies, sports, pets, ethnic food, and ugly people. Interested? Of course you are. Send me your photo, a copy of your last paycheck, and your university grades.

A. Discussion
1. How would you compare Luscious and Lonely to Action Man? Who do you think is better or worse? What are your reasons? How could they improve their profiles?
2. How would you compare Moon Unit to The Manager? Who do you think is better or worse? What are your reasons? How could they improve their profiles?

B. Writing
Rewrite one of the personal ads above to make it sound more appealing. Then write your own personal ad.

04
Struggles
Personal and Social Adversity

Objectives:
/ Make suggestions and demands
/ Listen to a story about time management
/ Give advice using should, could, had better

WARM UP

What advice do you give to someone who…?

- broke their leg
- got married
- won the lottery
- got dumped
- won a free trip to Hawaii
- got fired

IDIOMS

- **look on the bright side**
  A: I can't believe I failed that exam. I studied so hard!
  B: Well, *look on the bright side*. At least it's over.

- **dead end**
  I've been working at this company for five years. I have never been given a promotion! This job is such *a dead end*.

COLLOCATIONS

- **make mistakes**
  Everybody *makes mistakes* when they are learning a new language.

- **take the easy way out**
  A: My girlfriend and I get into so many fights! I should break up with her.
  B: Isn't that *taking the easy way out*?

LESSON 1

A. What Do You Recommend?

Language Point : Making Suggestions and Demands

The following verbs are used to stress importance or urgency:

demand She *demanded* (that) he *come* home earlier. **insist** I *insisted* (that) they *have* dinner at my house.	**suggest** I *suggest* (that) you *drink* plenty of water when it is hot outside. **recommend** The teacher *recommends* (that) she *study* the first five chapters before the exam tomorrow.

◇ Note: Use the base form of the verb in the clause that follows demand, insist, recommend, suggest

Part 1 ● With a partner, match the problems on the left with the appropriate suggestion or demand on the right.

1 The police officer **pulled me over** for speeding.
2 Tim asked his sister for advice about losing weight.
3 My mother went to see her doctor because she has been sick for over a week.
4 I went on a date with my boyfriend last night.
5 Fred went shopping with his friend Todd to buy a birthday present for his girlfriend.
6 The kindergarten students were shouting and throwing crayons at each other in the classroom.

a Their teacher demanded that they be nice to one another.
b Todd recommended he buy a pair of earrings.
c She suggested he go to the gym four times a week.
d He insisted he pay for dinner.
e He demanded that I pay $100 and gave me a ticket.
f He recommended that she get a lot of rest and drink plenty of water.

pull someone over *(phrase)*: to force someone to move to the side of the road

Part 2

Practice using insist, demand, recommend, and suggest to describe what is happening in the pictures below.

> **Example:**
> It looks like Grandpa was driving too fast. The police officer **demanded** that he **drive** slower and **be** careful.

1. Timmy and his teacher
2. Lisa and her Doctor
3. Cheryl and a Car Dealer
4. Jack, his date, and a bartender

B. What's On Your Plate?

Pre-listening

1. How many things below do you have **on your plate**?
   - Job
   - Hobbies
   - Family
   - Volunteering
   - School work
   - Friends

2. Have you ever accidentally **double-booked** a day or time? What happened?

3. Make predictions about what you think Lisa might have on her plate.

Listening TRACK 8-9

Listen to the dialogue about Lisa and her schedule problems for Thursday night.

Post-listening

Part 1 • Discuss what happened in the story. What is the problem? What do you think her **priority** should be? Why?

Part 2 •
Prioritize the following areas of your life from most to least important.

1
4
5
6
8
7
3
2

a. **Work**
b. **Family**
c. **Religion**
d. **Money**
e. **Friends**
f. **Love Life**
g. **Education**
h. **Health**

Discuss why you chose the order of your priorities and why certain things are more or less important to you.

on your plate *(idiom)*: things you have to get done
double-booked *(idiom)*: conflicting plans for the same time
priority *(noun)*: thing of greatest importance

Unit 4 Struggles | 63

C. What Would You Do?

Language Point : Giving Advice

The words had better, should, and could are used to give advice.

had better
to give strong advice and warnings that imply potential bad results

Example: *You'd better slow down! There's a police car behind us.*

should
to make a suggestion or give advice

Example: *You should really see a doctor about your headache.*

could
to make a suggestion or give options

Example: *You could buy a travel guide or you could take a tour.*

Agreeing and Disagreeing with Advice

Agreeing	Disagreeing
I think that's a good idea.	It's a good idea, but…
I agree!	I disagree because…
I see what you're saying.	The problem with that is…

1 You are having the following problems. Ask for advice.

2 Accept or reject your partner's advice.

3 If your partner rejects your advice, give them another option.

Example: You want to lose five kilograms.

A: *I want to lose five kilos by the end of the month. What do you think I **should** do?*

B: *OK. Well, what do you usually eat?*

A: *I eat cereal for breakfast, cookies for lunch, and ice cream for dinner. I don't know why I've gained so much weight!*

C: *You **could** start eating more vegetables and fruit. You **shouldn't** eat so much junk food!*

STUDENT A

3rd wheel
If you are the third wheel in this conversation, offer an alternative suggestion to the person seeking advice.

1. You need to buy a gift for a friend who just moved into his new home.

2. Your best friend is drinking too much alcohol these days.

3. You want to ask your boss for a raise.

4. Your parents do not like the person you want to marry.

5. You want to date one of your classmates.

6. You are stressed out from work.

7. You lost your wallet.

8. You think your boyfriend/girlfriend is **cheating on** you.

9. You do not know if you should finish school or get a job.

10. You have a toothache.

STUDENT B

1. You borrowed your friend's car and got into a car accident.
2. Your report that is due today is on your computer, but your computer is not working.
3. Your professor asked you out on a date.
4. You need to buy a present for your sister's birthday.
5. You do not know where to go on your next vacation.
6. You told a friend that you would help him with his homework, but now you cannot.
7. Your mom's cooking seems to be getting **bland**.
8. You are living overseas and miss your friends and family.
9. Your **fiancé(e)** wants a big wedding, but you want a small one.
10. You just received a love letter from someone you do not like.

cheat on *(v.)*: be unfaithful; have a relationship with someone else
bland *(adj.)*: having no flavor
fiancé *(n.)*: man engaged to be married, **fiancée**-woman engaged to be married

Discussion Questions

1. Are you the kind of person who complains if you are not happy about something, or do you just accept the situation?
   - Why do you think you are this way?

2. When was the last time you made a mistake?
   - What happened?
   - How did you deal with the situation?

3. If you do not like someone's suggestions or recommendations, is it better to tell him/her directly or just say nothing?
   - Why do you think so?

4. Could you recommend a good movie, show, or event you have seen recently?
   - What made you like it?

5. My friend is afraid of public speaking and has to give a presentation in two days. How would you suggest trying to overcome this fear?

6. What is your worst fear?
   - How do you think you can overcome this fear?

7. A friend of yours wants to join your English class but has a fear of making mistakes in front of other people. What would you tell your friend to convince him/her to join your class?

Unit 4 Struggles

LESSON 2

>> WARM UP
Look at the photos below and discuss the following:

> What happened?
> What do recommend he/she do to solve the problem?
> How do you think they feel in this situation?

Objectives:
/ Describe feelings with –ed and -ing

Office Worker

Victim

Student

Teenager

A. How Do You Feel?

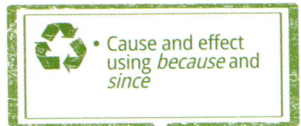
Cause and effect using *because* and *since*

Language Point : Describing Feelings and Emotions

Participial adjectives that end in –ed describe how a person feels.

Example:
*After realizing his pants had split, he was very **embarrassed**.*
*He was **confused** by her directions to the bank.*
*She was **disappointed** in her teammate's laziness.*

Part 1 ● Fill in the blanks with an adjective from the box.

- How do these people feel?
- Why do they feel this way?
- When was the last time you felt this way?

flattered	excited	confused
disgusted	frightened	shocked
amused	frustrated	embarrassed

Unit 4 Struggles | 69

Part 2

Language Point: Describing Situations

Participial adjectives that end in -ing are used to describe our opinions of situations and things.

> **Example:**
> *Falling over in front of a lot of people was **embarrassing**.*
> *My third-year calculus class is so **confusing**.*
> *Her speech was very **disappointing**.*

Describe your opinion of the following situations. Use the adjectives in the box below to help, or think of another adjective that best describes the situation.

How would you describe the following situations? Why?

1. speaking English with a native speaker
2. falling down on a crowded street
3. getting a high score on an exam
4. waiting in a long line for the subway
5. getting concert tickets to see your favorite musician or band
6. giving a presentation
7. watching a documentary
8. hiking to the top of a mountain
9. breaking up with a boyfriend or girlfriend
10. meeting your favorite celebrity

Terrifying	Amazing	Exciting
Heartbreaking	Thrilling	Exhausting
Frustrating	Interesting	Boring
Embarrassing	Worrying	Annoying

heartbreaking *(adj.):* making you feel very sad or upset.
* does not come from verb

B. What Have You Done For Me Lately?

Part 1 ● Look at each of the following statements and fill in the blank. Use the pictures as a guide to help you find the right word for the statement. Then change the word into an adjective ending in –ed or –ing.

> bore, exhaust, thrill, embarrass, shock, excite, worry, disgust, confuse, annoy, frustrate, amaze

Find someone who.......

... has seen a __ (boring) __ movie recently.

... is _____ about their future.

... thinks mosquitoes are _____.

... is _____ by technology.

... is _____ when skiing or snowboarding.

... feels _____ by their job.

... was _____ when studying for an exam.

... was _____ when their team won a big game.

... thinks dating is _____.

... thinks speaking in front of people is _____.

... was _____ when riding the subway.

... has eaten something _____.

Part 2 ● Interview your classmates to find out if they have been in these situations and why they felt that way.

> **Example:**
> **A:** *Have you seen a boring movie recently?*
> **B:** *Yes, I have.*
> **C:** *Why did you think it was so boring?*
> **A:** *I was really bored because the main characters just talked the whole time.*

C. Who Are You? Who, Who? Who, Who?

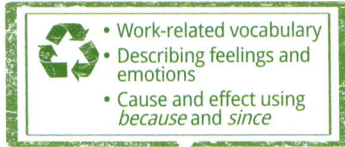
- Work-related vocabulary
- Describing feelings and emotions
- Cause and effect using *because* and *since*

Part 1 ● Invent a new you! Make up answers to the following questions to create a character. Be specific and make sure to remember your answers.

1. What is your new name? Do you have a nickname? How do you feel about your nickname?
2. What is your nationality? What do you think about life in your country?
3. What is your job? How long have you worked there? How do you feel about your job?
4. You have a pet. What is it? What does it look like? What kind of personality does it have?
5. You have a very special talent or ability. What is it?

Part 2 ● Discuss the following questions. What would your character from Part 1 do in these situations?

1a. You come home and your front door is open. How do you feel? What do you do?

1b. The house appears to be empty. Nothing is stolen or even moved. How do you feel? What could have caused the door to be open?

2a. You have spent all day preparing a **lavish** meal for your significant other. What is it? It is very delicious. How do you feel about the meal you have prepared?

2b. You step out of the room for a few minutes. When you return, your pet has jumped on the table and eaten everything. How do you feel? What do you do?

3a. You have received a promotion. What would your promotion be in your line of work? How do you feel about your promotion?

3b. You have told everyone about your new job and have a huge party to celebrate. How do you celebrate? How would you describe the celebration?

3c. The next day you receive an email from your boss. The company is downsizing. You are going to be laid off. How do you feel about the situation?

4a. The mayor calls. The city is under attack from the giant koala monster, Koazilla. How do you feel? How can your special talent or ability save the city?

4b. You defeat Koazilla after a long and difficult fight. How do you feel?

lavish (adj.): using a large amount of something

Discussion Questions

1. What kinds of things **stress you out**?
   ▶ What are some good ways to relieve stress?

2. Do you think you are the kind of person who is easily frustrated?
   ▶ Why or why not?

3. When was the last time you felt **overwhelmed**?
   ▶ What happened?

4. Have you heard any surprising news lately?
   ▶ What was the news and why were you surprised?

5. What kinds of things or people inspire you?
   ▶ Why do they make you feel inspired?

6. What kind of behavior do you find disgusting?
   ▶ Why does this behavior disgust you?

7. How would you feel if you saw a thief steal someone's wallet?
   ▶ What would you do in this situation?

8. What are you concerned about in today's world?
   ▶ Why do these things concern you?

UNIT 4 REVIEW

How well can you:
- ☐ Make suggestions and demands?
- ☐ Give advice?
- ☐ Describe feelings and emotions?

What do you need to study more?

stress out *(phrasal verb)*: to suffer from mental stress
overwhelmed *(adj.)*: to have to many problems to deal with

Activity: I Wish I May, I Wish I Might

Imagine you have just found a magical SLE textbook. After rubbing the book, your partner appears as a genie who can grant three wishes; however, there are three kinds of wishes that the genie cannot **fulfill**:

1. The genie can't make anyone fall in love with you.
2. You can't wish for more wishes.
3. The genie can't grant you a free trip to SLE Level 3A.

In addition to telling the genie your wishes, you should also explain why you want to have your wishes fulfilled. After you have had a chance to talk about it with your partner, share your wishes with the class.

74 | SLE Generations 2A

fulfill *(v.)*: satisfy something

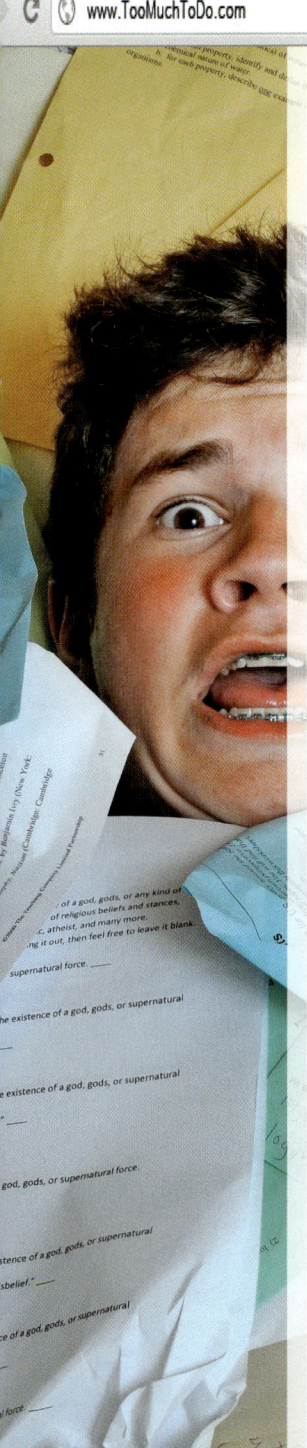

WORLD FORUM

Segue TooMuchToDo.com

Home   Discussions   General   Welcome to our new Forum   Search

Too Much To Do

help-me-lisa
AArrghh! I'm so frustrated! I never seem to be able to stick to a schedule. All of this double-booking is making me exhausted. Trying to help everybody and finish everything on my plate is so darn tiring. What would you recommend for someone who is very overwhelmed?

WandaB.Hepful
I used to have such similar problems. I was always worried I would forget to be somewhere. It was so humiliating when someone would text me asking, "Where R U?" and I had no idea we had an appointment. You should stop making any commitments! Worked for me!

Dr Time
I would recommend that you prioritize your tasks and commitments using a number scale in a day planner. Get in the habit of writing everything down and assigning it a number between 1 and 5. Then before you commit to anything, you have an easy way to decide what is most important to you. This will feel a lot less overwhelming.

Spambot1000
Time? Time shares in Siberia! Cheap4U Prescriptions. Follow link. http//:www.annoyingyoutonoend.com/goawayanddie

A. Discussion
1. Who do you think gives Lisa the best and worst advice? Why?
2. Do you tend to feel stressed by your schedule or do you feel relaxed?
3. Have you ever had a time conflict between family and friends? Which commitment was more important to you?

B. Writing:
Tell Lisa about a time you felt like you were in a similar situation and give her some advice about what she could do to fix it.

Unit 4 Struggles | 75

05
There and Back Again
Travel and Transportation

Objectives:
/ Make decisions and choices about travel
/ Listen to a discussion about a trip

WARM UP

A. Discuss how you get to the following places. Be sure to be as specific as possible and ask follow-up questions.

> **How do you get to…**
>
> …your house from this class?
>
> …your office or university from home?
>
> …the nearest city from this city?

B. List as many forms of transportation as you can think of in the world. Which do you prefer? Why?

IDIOMS

- **in the same boat**
  We're both stuck in traffic and late for work. It looks like we're *in the same boat*.
- **hit the road**
  It's getting really late I'd better *hit the road*.

COLLOCATIONS

- **take a holiday**
  We're *taking a holiday* to Spain.
- **go on a vacation**
  We're *going on a vacation* to Spain.

What Is It?

Explain the meaning with your partner.
- a guided tour
- to go sightseeing
- to book a ticket
- a layover

Unit 5 There and Back Again | 77

LESSON 1

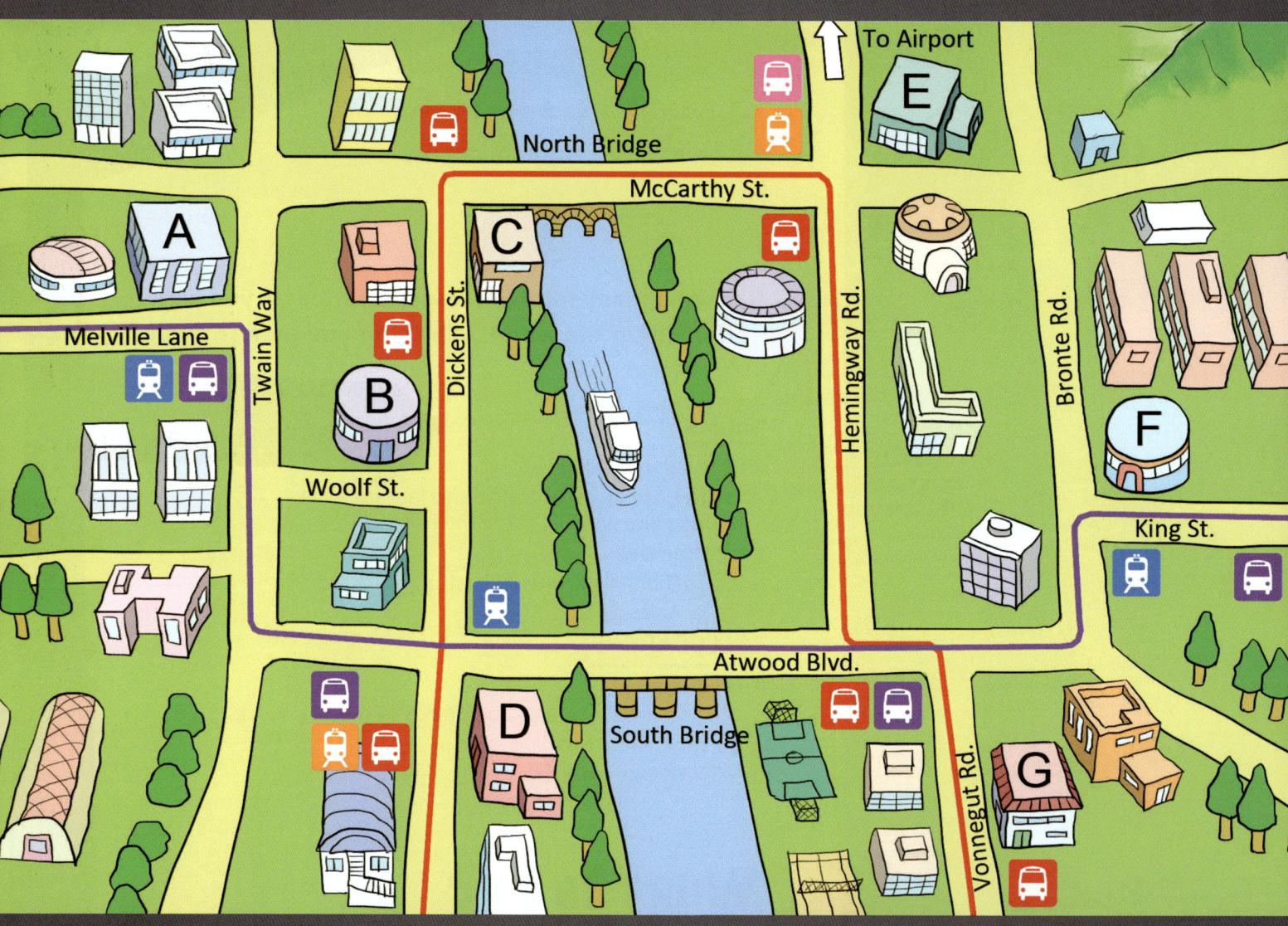

- **A** TechnoElectronic World
- **B** Special Kitty Day Care
- **C** The Daily Coffee Shop
- **D** Chapter 11 Bookstore
- **E** Fresh Family Grocery
- **F** Wok World Chinese Restaurant
- **G** The Thompson Home

Subway Station = Blue Line and Orange Line
Airport Shuttle = Pink Bus
Bus Stops and Route = Red Bus and Purple Bus

Did You Know?
"Get in" vs. "Get on"

These two phrasal verbs are very similar! When talking about travel, "get on" is generally used for vehicles in which you can stand, and "get in" is used for vehicles in which you must sit.

A. In a Rush

Answer the following questions by giving the most appropriate directions from the map provided.

1 In your own car, what is the best way to get from Special Kitty Day Care to Wok World Chinese Restaurant?

2 What is the best way to get from TechnoElectronic World to Fresh Family Grocery using only public transportation?

3 Sally needs to get from Techno Electronic World to Chapter 11 Bookstore. She has lost her wallet, so she will have to walk.

• What is the fastest way for Sally to get to the bookstore?

4 Biff is driving Lisa home after their date, but he wants to spend as much time with her as he can.

• What is the slowest route Bift can take from the Daily Coffee Shop to the family home?

Need to Know:

- **to take a (taxi), to take a (left/right)**

  Why don't you **take a taxi** instead of the subway?

  When you get to Main Street, **take a left** on Melrose.

- **to get on a (bus/plane)**

  We **got on the bus** just outside the Museum of Modern Art.

- **to change (buses)**

  You will need **to change buses** at the library.

- **to transfer (subway lines)**

  When you get to City Station, you will need to **transfer** to Line 7.

---

5 Frick and Frack are distributing flyers to all of the local businesses.

• How can they go to each business without having to **backtrack**?

6 The Thompsons are running late to the airport. It's the middle of **rush hour** and there is a major traffic jam on both Hemmingway Rd. and Bronte Rd.

• What is their quickest route?

7 Jack arrives home after class, and he finds a list of things his mother wants him to pick up before dinner. He needs to get a book his father ordered from the bookstore and some cat food for Mr. Squiggles. The North Bridge is closed for the afternoon.

• What is the best way for Jack to take?

---

backtrack *(v.)*: to return the same way you came
rush hour *(n.)*: the busiest time for traffic before and after work

B. Bears, Bears, Bears

Pre-listening

1. Do you prefer relaxing and restful vacations or vacations full of action and excitement?
   - What was the last restful or exciting vacation you took?

Now look at the picture below. Make predictions about what you think is happening in this situation.

2. Who wants to go where?
   - Do they all agree?
   - What kind of vacations are each of them hoping for?

Listening TRACK 10-11

After listening, look back at Question 2 and discuss how close your predictions were to the dialogue.

Post-listening

Mark the following statements based on the listening with True (T), False (F), or if there is not enough information as a question mark (?). If the answer is False, make it into a true statement.

1	T ☐ F ☐ ? ☐	The family is planning their winter vacation.
2	T ☐ F ☐ ? ☐	Richard and Susan want to go on a cruise.
3	T ☐ F ☐ ? ☐	Lisa thinks there is a lot to do on a cruise ship.
4	T ☐ F ☐ ? ☐	The cruise offers chances to gamble, golf, and see theatre.
5	T ☐ F ☐ ? ☐	Susan likes her daughter's idea of going skydiving.
6	T ☐ F ☐ ? ☐	Jack wants to go camping in the mountains.
7	T ☐ F ☐ ? ☐	Richard took Jack and Lisa camping last year.
8	T ☐ F ☐ ? ☐	The cruise ship is full of bears.

Unit 5 There and Back Again | 81

C. When in Rome...or is that Egypt?

Making recommendations and suggestions
Giving advice
Comparisons

Part 1

Rank the following items in order of importance (1=Most important, 6=Least important) when choosing a summer vacation destination:

- **Food**
- **Temperature**
- **Shopping**
- **Popular tourist attractions**
- **Cost**
- **Distance from home**

Compare your ranking with a partner and ask follow-up questions.

> **Example:**
>
> **A:** *I think tourist attractions are the most important part of a vacation.*
>
> **B:** *Oh, I think food is the most important part. Why do you think the number of tourist attractions is so important?*
>
> **A:** *I really love to take pictures when I go on vacation.*

Part 2

You want to go on summer vacation together for a week, but you do not know where to go. Your budget for the week is $900. Look at the country profiles below and choose <u>one</u> destination. Make sure to <u>compare</u> your options and ask follow-up questions.

> **Example:**
>
> **A:** *We need to take a vacation! Where do you think we should go?*
>
> **B:** *Well, what types of activities do you enjoy in the summer?*
>
> **A:** *I really like to take walks and go surfing.*
>
> **B:** *OK. Maybe we could go to Costa Rica or Iceland.*
>
> **A:** *Hmmm...the temperature in Iceland might be cold. How about Kenya? The hotel cost is cheaper than the hotel in Costa Rica.*

Cairo, Egypt

Hotel Cost: $250 for the week
Temperature: 45°C
Activities: (for one person)
- Go to the Cairo International Film Festival, $40
- Go on a Pyramid tour, $20
- Go on a Nile River dinner cruise, $30

Food: $15 for one meal

Tokyo, Japan

Hotel Cost: $490 for the week
Temperature: 33°C
Activities: (for one person)
- Visit Tokyo Disney, $60
- Go to a Japanese garden, $8
- Visit Tokyo Sky Tree, $10

Food: $30 for one meal

Edinburgh, Scotland

Hotel Cost: $400 for the week
Temperature: 20°C
Activities: (for one person)
- Visit Edinburgh Castle, $20
- Watch a performance at Edinburgh Festival Theatre, $15
- Go shopping on Princes Street, $100

Food: $20 for one meal

Nairobi, Kenya

Hotel Cost: $150 for the week
Temperature: 40°C
Activities: (for one person)
- Visit Langata Giraffe Centre, $20
- Go shopping at the Village Market, $50
- Visit traditional tribal villages, $15

Food: $5 for one meal

San Jose, Costa Rica

Hotel Cost: $200 for the week
Temperature: 27°C
Activities: (for one person)
- Go on a rainforest tour, $20
- Take surfing lessons, $15
- Go horseback riding, $20
- Go river rafting, $15

Food: $10 for one meal

Reykjavík, Iceland

Hotel Cost: $300 for the week
Temperature: 18°C
Activities: (for one person)
- Go whale watching, $200
- Viking museum $10
- Go hiking, free
- Going to the beach, free
- Enjoying hot springs, $15

Food: $25 for one meal

Athens, Greece

Hotel Cost: $200 for the week
Temperature: 40°C
Activities: (for one person)
- Visit Greek temples, $15
- Go to the Athens Municipal Art Gallery, $25
- Visit site of the first Olympic games, $10

Food: $30 for one meal

Atlanta, Georgia

Hotel Cost: $300 for the week
Temperature: 32°C
Activities: (for one person)
- Visit Coca-Cola headquarters, $10
- Visit Georgia Aquarium (world's largest indoor aquarium), $20
- Watch a performance at Centennial Olympic Park, $15

Food: $15 for one meal

Discussion Questions

1. What is your preferred type of public transportation?
   ▶ Which form of public transportation is your least favorite?

2. What was the most recent trip you took?
   ▶ How did you get there and what kinds of transportation did you use?
   ▶ How long did the trip take?
   ▶ What about the cost, weather, and activities?

3. What are the advantages and disadvantages of owning your own car?

4. Where would you most like to travel to?
   ▶ Why would you like to go there?

5. Have you ever traveled to another city or country that you prefer over your own?
   ▶ Would you prefer to live in that place?
   ▶ If not, why do you think your city or country is the best place to live?

6. How do you think travel and transportation will change in the next 20 years?

7. When foreign friends visit your country, what do you suggest that they see and do?
   ▶ Why would you recommend these sights and activities?
   ▶ How would you suggest they get around?

LESSON 2

>> WARM UP
Look at the following international traffic signs and discuss what you think the meaning is for each.

Objectives:
/ Talk about likely and unlikely situations with conditionals

A. What Will Happen If...

> **Language Point:** Expressing Likely and Unlikely Possibilities with Conditionals

To express likely possibilities:

> if + present tense, + will + verb

Example
- *If it rains*, *I will get* wet.
- *I will be able to buy* my dream car *if I get* this job.

To express unlikely events or unreal circumstances:

> if + simple past tense, + would/could + verb

Example
- *If you won* the lottery, you *could go* on a cruise to the Bahamas.
- *I would fly* to Paris *if I were* a bird.

◇ Note: '*were*' is used for both singular and plural subjects.

Match the following sentence halves to make complete sentences. Say whether you agree or disagree with the statements.

Real Situations

1 If I lose my wallet ...
2 You will get lost in Seoul ...
3 You will arrive at your destination faster...
4 If a tourist loses his passport...
5 Airfare will be cheaper...

a ... he will not be able to leave the country.
b ... if you **book** the tickets in advance.
c ... if you take the express train.
d ... if you do not speak Korean.
e ... I will have to call the credit card company.

Unreal Situations

1 If you went to Paris...
2 If we got into a car accident...
3 If the airline lost my luggage...
4 You could get a sunburn ...
5 If you remembered to bring your swim suit...

a ...we would have to walk home.
b ...I would not have any clothes to wear.
c ... you could go swimming.
d ...you would need to be fluent in French.
e ... if you weren't wearing **sunscreen**.

book *(v.)*: to make a reservation for a hotel, restaurant, etc.
sunscreen *(n.)*: lotion put on the skin to prevent sunburn

B. If I Had My Way

Practice talking about unlikely possibilities by completing the sentences. Remember to ask follow-up questions.

> **Example:**
> **A:** *If I were rich, I would buy an apartment in London.*
> **B:** *Where in London would you want to live?*

If I got a new pet…

…if I studied English every day.

…… if it snowed next week.

If I were given plane tickets to go anywhere…

If our teacher quit his/her job in the middle of class…

If I had my favorite celebrity over for dinner…

If I could change one thing about myself…

…if a large meteor from space were going to destroy the planet in ten days.

C. A Three-Hour Tour

Part 1 ● The Thompson family is out to sea and suddenly the yacht they are sailing on begins to sink! They only have time to take five items from the ship and safely get to a nearby island. Decide which items they should take with them. Remember, they could be on the island for many weeks or months!

> **Example:** *If they **take** the volleyball, they **won't** get bored.*

Part 2 • On This Island

You're stranded on the island with the Thompson Family! What would you do in the following situations? The only items you have available are what you chose in Part 1 and things you might find on a desert island.

1. You need a place to rest but the ground on the island is very rocky and uncomfortable. *I would…….*

2. It's the middle of the night. You hear a strange sound in the woods.

3. You find the source of the sound – it's a large wild pig. He runs at you!

4. You are getting hungry on the island. You find a banana tree, but there is a **raging** river between you and it.

5. You find a few chickens, but if you decide to kill them and eat them raw, you might get very sick.

6. You meet a tribe of **cannibals** who don't understand your language. They look hungry.

7. One night, a very big storm comes. It starts **raining cats and dogs**.

8. You see a ship on the **horizon**. If you get their attention, you can go home!

raging *(adj.)*: very strong
cannibal *(n)*: an animal that eats its own kind
raining cats and dogs *(idiom)*: raining very hard
horizon *(n.)*: the line where the earth meets the sky

Discussion Questions

1 If you were an animal, what would you be?

2 If you could only wear one piece of clothing, what would it be?

3 If you had a time machine, when and where would you go?

4 What would you do if you found a wallet on the street? Why?

5 If you had to lose one of your five senses, which one would you lose?

6 If you could only eat one type of meal for the rest of your life, what would it be?

7 If you had the power to change three things about the world, what would you change?

8 What would you do if you could be **invisible** for one day?

9 If you could choose to have a son or daughter, which would you choose and why?

UNIT 5 REVIEW

How well can you use:
- ☐ travel and transportation vocabulary?
- ☐ expressing likely and unlikely possibilities?
- ☐ decision making skills?

What do you need to study more?

invisible *(adj)*: unable to be seen

Activity: Riddle-de-dum

The Problem:

A man has to get a fox, a chicken, and a sack of corn across a river. He has a rowboat, but it can only carry him and one other thing.

If the fox and the chicken are left together, the fox will eat the chicken.

If the chicken and the corn are left together, the chicken will eat the corn.

How does the man do it?

HINT !

Some items might have to cross the river more than once.

While solving the riddle

Ask your partners:
- What would happen if the man took the _____ first?
- What would happen if the man took the _____ next?

Family Rescued on Desert Island

By **Lawson D. Woods**, PNN

In a dramatic story of survival, the Thompson family was rescued from a previously unknown island yesterday. The Thompsons got on a small tour boat during their vacation, which sank an hour later. The family was mostly unhurt, well fed, and appeared happy.

The family managed to survive their six-week ordeal with only five items they salvaged from the sinking ship. "Lisa suggested if we brought the sleeping bags we would be comfortable." said Jack Thompson.

It wasn't just a bad night's sleep the Thompsons had to deal with. "Dad recommended that if we brought the gun we could protect ourselves. A good idea because a wild pig attacked our camp," said Lisa Thompson, "and mom brought the rope. Because she brought the rope, we could cross that river for the bananas!"

The Thompsons, however, were not alone. The island was also populated by cannibals. "It was Lisa that saved us," said mom. She claimed if we brought the novel, we could read aloud. It turns out the cannibals love having Harry Potter read to them even though they can't understand our language. Who knew? The Thompsons plan on returning home to their cat, Mr. Squiggles, and never going on a cruise again.

A. Discussion
1. What items did the family bring with them?
   Why did they bring each one?
   Were these the same items you chose to bring?
2. Do you think it would be possible for you to survive out in the wilderness for several weeks or more?
   Why do you think so?
3. If you could choose to go somewhere and be alone for a month, where would you go?

B. Writing
Write a short paragraph telling the story from another character's perspective. For example, one of the tour boat operators, the rescuers, or even one of the cannibals.

WARM UP

What chores have you done recently?
Who does these things in your house?

- do the dishes
- fold the laundry
- take the trash out
- pay the bills
- cook dinner
- clean the bathroom

What are some things other people have done for you recently?

PHRASAL VERBS

- **get up**
- **sleep in**
  I have to *get up* every day at six, so this weekend I'm *sleeping in*.
- **clean up**
  We had a big party last night, and the house needs to be *cleaned up*.

COLLOCATIONS

- **Check my teeth/eyes/health**
- **run errands**
  I have to *run* a lot of *errands* today and get my *eyes checked*.

IDIOMS

- **at the crack of dawn**
  My uncle goes to work at the *crack of dawn*.
- **run like clockwork**
  I have to get my car serviced every three months, but after that it *runs like clockwork*.

Unit 6 A Day in the Life | 95

LESSON 1

A. Who Kicked Mr. Squiggles?

Language Point: Passive Voice

Active Voice
Simple active sentences say the subject does something to the object.
Who kicked Mr. Squiggles?

Bill is the focus of the sentence and the one doing the action.

subject	verb	object
Bill	kicked	Mr. Squiggles.

Passive Voice
What if we do not know who performed the action? Mr. Squiggles becomes the subject. Who performed the action is not important.
What happened to Mr. Squiggles?

subject	to be + past participle	object
Mr. Squiggles.	was kicked	(unknown)

A passive sentence can also include the phrase **(by+someone)**. This is to make it understood that it was Bill who performed the action and not Ted.
Mr. Squiggles was kicked by Bill.

subject	to be + past participle	by + object
Mr. Squiggles.	was kicked	by Bill.

◆ Note: Only verbs that are transitive (verbs that can take an object) can be used in the passive. Intransitive verbs cannot be used in passive sentences.

Example: *I slept for eight hours last night. I got up at ten o'clock.*

1 Change these forms into passive questions. Ask and answer the questions. Ask follow up questions.

> **Who/service/your family car**
>
> **A:** *Who is your car serviced by?*
> **B:** *My car is serviced by Fonzi's garage.*
> **A:** *How often do you take your car there for service?*

1. Who / make / the best coffee
2. Where / sell / good quality clothes
3. Who / write / your favorite book
4. Who / make / the best pizza
5. When / celebrate / your favorite holiday
6. Who / make / your shoes
7. Who / cut / your hair
8. Who / check / your teeth

2 Describe Mr. Squiggles' typical day using both the active and passive voice.

> **A:** *Jack **plays** with Mr. Squiggles in the morning. What happens after that?*
> **B:** *Mr. Squiggles **feels exhausted** by the fun.*

Mr. Squiggles' typical day

Unit 6 A Day in the Life | 97

B. The Case of the Consumed Cream Cake

Susan spent two days making a very special cake. On Monday night at 7 p.m., she left the house to run a few **errands**. When she returned at 8 p.m., half of the cake had been eaten! She called a meeting of everyone in the house, but nobody admitted responsibility.

Listening TRACK 12-13

As you listen, fill in the chart to find out who might have committed the crime.

errand *(n.)*: small job to collect or deliver something
narrow down *(phrasal v.)*: to limit the amount of things being considered

	Richard (Husband)	Lisa (Daughter)	Jack (Son)	Martha and Charles (In-laws)	Mr. Squiggles (Cat)
At home during the time of the crime					
Doesn't like strawberry					
Has brown hair					
Found with icing on them					

Post-listening

Now that you've **narrowed down** the suspects, here are a few more clues:

cat food cans lying on the floor

Scratches on the table

Unopened snacks on the table

Looking at the new clues and the information you collected from the chart above, discuss:
• who you think is the most likely suspect and
• why they did it

Unit 6 A Day in the Life | 99

C. I Said Hey, What's Going On?

- Past progressive
- Because and Since

Look at the picture and start with what happened. Then, use the verbs below to explain how the story happened in reverse. Try to use as many verbs as you can in each story.

Example:
A: *The dog's leg was broken by a scooter.* **Why?**
B: *Because he was chasing Mr. Squiggles down the street.* **Why?**
C: *Since his food was stolen by Mr. Squiggles.* **Why?**

spill
throw out
fall
cut
knock over
catch
ruin
slap
smash

Discussion Questions

1 What kinds of things do you do every day?
   ▶ How about once a month?

2 What time have you been getting up and going to bed recently?
   ▶ What do you think the advantages and disadvantages of being a morning or a night person are?

3 What do you usually have for breakfast?
   ▶ Who makes your breakfast every morning?

4 Who does the following chores in your house: (answer with passive voice)
   ▶ do the dishes
   ▶ fold the laundry
   ▶ take the trash out
   ▶ mop the floor
   ▶ cook dinner
   ▶ clean the bathroom

5 Are you pretty good at **sticking to a schedule**, or do you usually **run late**?
   ▶ Why?

6 What personal activities (hobbies, sports, interests) do you make a part of your daily routine?
   ▶ How do feel when you don't have time for them?

7 Do you usually wake up at the **crack of dawn**, or do you **sleep in**?
   ▶ Why? What are the advantages and disadvantages of each?

sticking to a schedule *(idiom)*: following a routine closely
run late *(idiom)*: not coming at a scheduled time
crack of dawn *(idiom)*: very early in the morning
sleep in *(phrasal v.)*: sleep late into the day

Unit 6 A Day in the Life | 101

LESSON 2

>> WARM UP

Objectives:
/ Use causative passive
/ Review giving advice
/ Review likely and unlikely possibilities

Look at the pictures below and discuss the following questions:
> What things are done by these people at work?
> What skills do these people need for work?

water, arrange

cut, wash

serve, make

change, service

prepare, cook

A. Hotel Management

You are general managers in a hotel. The schedules for this week are incomplete. Ask questions using the active voice, and answer questions with the passive voice. Use the verbs next to the department name to help you form questions.

Example:

A: *Who will manage the front desk on Sunday?*
B: *The front desk **will be managed** by Matt on Sunday.*

A: *Who is going to cook the food on Wednesday?*
B: *The food **is going to be cooked** by Chef Jeremy on Wednesday.*

- Active vs. passive voice
- Future tense

STUDENT A

Department	Area	Sun.	Mon.	Tues.	Wed.	Thurs.	Fri.	Sat.
Front Desk	front desk (manage)	Matt		Lisa		Matt	Lisa	Matt
Housekeeping	rooms (clean)		Annette	Emilio	Carl	Annette		Emilio
Restaurant	restaurant (supervise)	Rod		Rod	Sarah		Sarah	Sarah
Bar	bar (staff)	Brian	Joseph	Hillary		Joseph	Hillary	
Kitchen	food (cook)	Chef Todd	Chef Jaime		Chef Jeremy		Chef Jeremy	Chef Rudy
Banquets	banquets (organize)	Jeff	Gary		David	Gary		Tony
Sales	rooms (sell)		Heather	Carolyn	Cheryl	Carolyn	Heather	

Unit 6 A Day in the Life | 103

STUDENT B

Department	Area	Sun.	Mon.	Tues.	Wed.	Thurs.	Fri.	Sat.
Front Desk	front desk (manage)	Matt	Valerie		Shirley		Lisa	Matt
Housekeeping	rooms (clean)	Annette		Emilio	Carl	Annette	Carl	
Restaurant	restaurant (supervise)		Brandon	Rod	Sarah	Rod		Sarah
Bar	bar (staff)	Brian	Joseph		Mason		Hillary	Hillary
Kitchen	food (cook)	Chef Todd	Chef Jaime	Chef Todd		Chef Rudy	Chef Jeremy	
Banquets	banquets (organize)			Tony	David	Gary	Jeff	Tony
Sales	rooms (sell)	Cheryl	Heather	Carolyn		Carolyn		Heather

3rd wheel

Write down the schedule as you hear it, checking that the information is correct as you go.

B. What a Beautiful Day in the Neighborhood

Language Point : Causative Passive

We can use this form to say we are having something done for us.
The person who pays for or orders the action is the subject of the sentence. Use either the verb "have" or "get" then a passive phrase as the object.

Subject	Verb	Object + Past Participle
I	get/have	my nails done by a manicurist.

PART 1 • Change the sentences to show that you caused something to happen using the causative passive and a by phrase to say who performed the action.

1 My car is serviced.

2 A pizza was delivered.

3 My suits are cleaned.

4 Our family portrait was taken.

5 My teeth are checked.

6 The dog was groomed.

PART 2 • When Susan and Richard first got married, they lived in a terrible neighborhood, but they **fixed up** their house and made it beautiful. Use the causative passive to describe what Richard or Susan had done and by whom. See if you can find at least 10 improvements.

Example:

A: What did Richard and Susan do with the lawn?
B: They had the grass cut by Larry's Lawn Service.

Possible verbs:

- Clean
- Fix
- Paint
- Pull
- Remove
- Replace
- Cut
- Install
- Plant
- Sweep
- Repair
- Water

People for hire:

- Larry's Lawn Service
- The Fence Doctor
- Handyman Harry
- Sunny Windows
- Part Time Painters
- A-1 Garage
- Green Gardeners
- Crime Busters CCTV
- Rascal Roofer

fix up *(phrasal v.)*: to repair or improve

C. Decisions, Decisions, Decisions...

Take turns asking for and giving advice for each of the following situations. Use language that you learned in Unit 5 and the passive voice in your questions and answers.

Example:

Getting a pet: fish, dog, alligator

A: *I'm thinking about **getting a pet** and need some advice. If you were me, would you get a fish, a dog, or an alligator?*

B: *I would get a fish. If you got a fish, you wouldn't need a big apartment. Also, fish **are fed** just once a day, so they are cheap. If you bought a dog, you would need more time and money because dogs **are fed** twice a day, and they have to be walked outside.*

STUDENT A

1 Getting a new job: police officer, tour guide, high school teacher

2 Being in a relationship: stay single forever, get married this year, get married 10 years from now

3 Going to work/school: bicycle, car, public transportation

4 Taking a vacation: going on an African safari, skiing in Canada, shopping in Paris

5 Breaking up with someone: over the phone, by letter, face to face

6 Going on a date: art museum, café, amusement park

7 Getting in shape: jogging, weight lifting, boxing

8 Eating dinner: cooking spaghetti, ordering pizza, going to a Chinese restaurant

STUDENT B

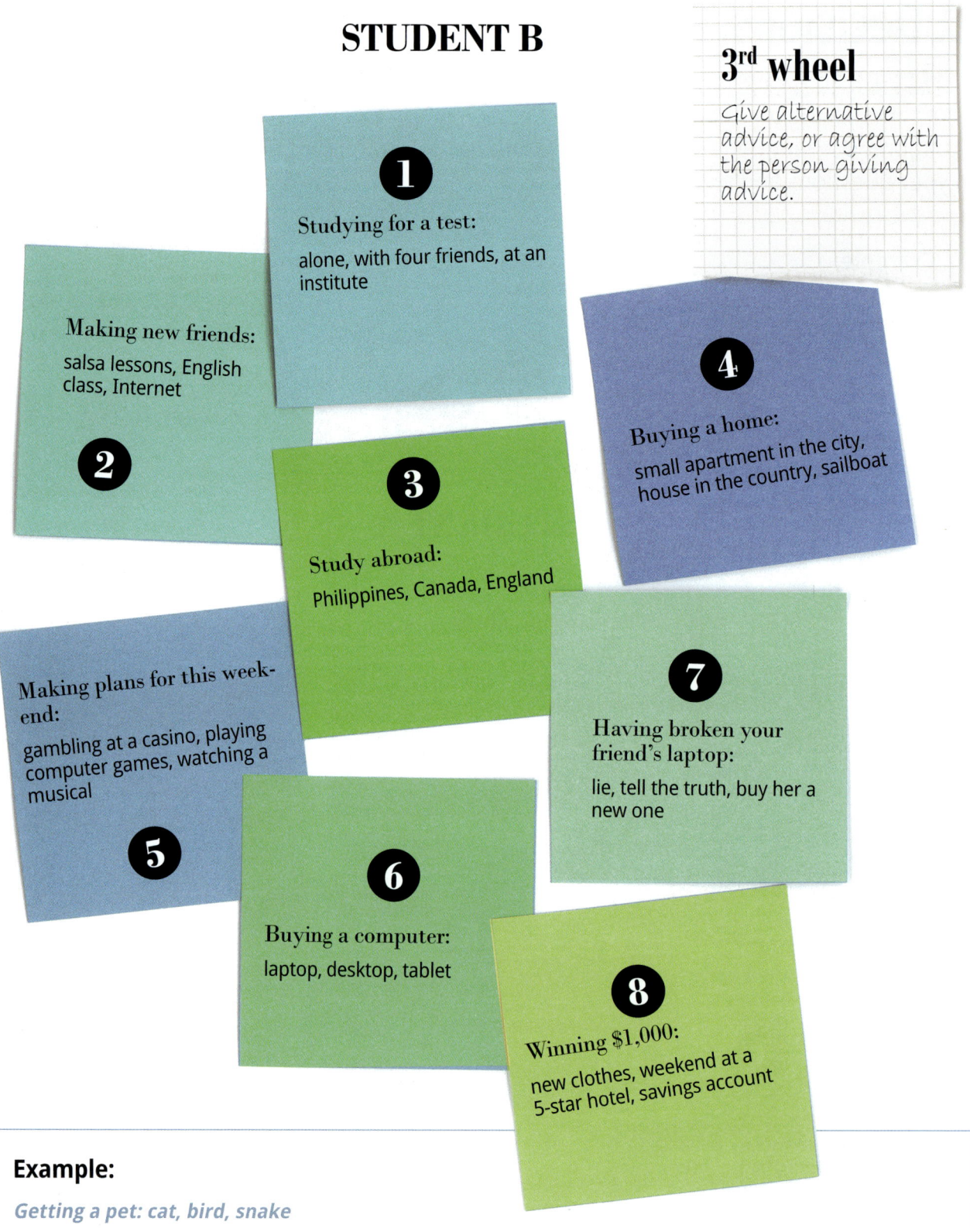

3rd wheel
Give alternative advice, or agree with the person giving advice.

1 Studying for a test: alone, with four friends, at an institute

2 Making new friends: salsa lessons, English class, Internet

3 Study abroad: Philippines, Canada, England

4 Buying a home: small apartment in the city, house in the country, sailboat

5 Making plans for this weekend: gambling at a casino, playing computer games, watching a musical

6 Buying a computer: laptop, desktop, tablet

7 Having broken your friend's laptop: lie, tell the truth, buy her a new one

8 Winning $1,000: new clothes, weekend at a 5-star hotel, savings account

Example:

Getting a pet: cat, bird, snake

A: *I'm thinking about **getting a pet** and need some advice. If you were me, would you get a cat, a bird, or a snake?*

B: *I would get a snake because snakes **are fed** only once a month. If you get a bird, you will have to take care of it forever because birds live so long.*

Discussion Questions

1 Have you ever had clothes made for you?
   ▶ What did you have made and for what occasion?
   ▶ If not, what would you like to have made?
2 Where do you usually go to have your hair cut?
   ▶ Why do you prefer that place to others?
3 When was the last time you had your photo taken professionally?
4 If you could have any one of the following services provided for you free of charge for a year, which would you choose and why?
   ▶ **chauffeuring**   ▶ house cleaning
   ▶ professional massage   ▶ hairstyling
   ▶ cooking by a chef   ▶ personal fitness trainer
5 If you had a robot that could perform various household chores and run errands, what would you have it do?
6 Have you ever had your fortune told?
   ▶ Do you believe in fortune tellers? Why or why not?
7 Have you ever **played a trick** on someone or had a trick played on you?
   ▶ What happened?
8 How often do have your teeth checked?
   ▶ How about your vision?
   ▶ How about your health?

UNIT 6 REVIEW

How well can you use:
☐ Active voice vs. Passive voice?
☐ Causative passive?
What do you need to study more?

chauffeuring *(n.)*: personal driving service
play a trick *(idiom)*: to trick someone into believing something as a joke

Activity: The Case of the Disappearing Family Man

A man named Sam Smith suddenly disappeared. He seemed happily married with two children and a good job at a bank. Everyone is confused. Where is he? Did he leave on his own? If so, why? Was he kidnapped? Look over the clues below, and try to figure out what happened. When you are done, present your version of the events to the rest of your class. See who came up with the best explanation for Sam's disappearance.

The following clues were found:

- Part of a handwritten note saying, "...never want to see you again...don't try to get in touch with me. Jane..."
- A $100 bill
- A page torn out of a phone book containing information about travel agencies
- A photo of a young woman wearing a bikini
- A photo of the same woman sitting on an office desk.
- Two symphony tickets for Wednesday evening at 8pm
- Another handwritten letter reading "...I know it's the coward's way out, but I really had no choice. You may not believe me, but I do still love you and only wish everything turned out..."
- A guidebook entitled, "Navigating the Seven Seas"
- A notice of resignation to take effect in two weeks
- An advertisement circled in red, reading "Yacht for Sale"
- A job advertisement for an accounts manager taken from a newspaper
- A company credit card with receipts for lunches, jewelry, hotel rooms, etc.

Segue

MyFaceWorld

Susan Thompson

strawberry cream cake stolen by family!
The cake was eaten by one of them this evening. I just know it! I was out having all the things done that we neglected on our overseas trip. When I came home, the kitchen had been destroyed by the thief. Only a single brown hair had been left as a clue. Both Lisa and Richard have brown hair, but Rich and Jack love strawberry. Decisions. Decisions.

Lisa T.
Oh Mom! Give it up. I told you that on my way home from the market I stopped to get my nails done. I was really hungry, but strawberry is so barf! I'm sure the cake was eaten by Jack. He's so lazy. The laundry wasn't done because he was probably stuffing his face.

The Jackster
Is your homework done, Sis? Ma, I didn't do it! Okay the laundry wasn't done, but I was distracted because the cat was already fed. He wasn't begging so we spent some time playing with a string. Besides it was Dad who went to bed not feeling very well.

Rich Thompson
Hold on Jack. I was out having my haircut and I bought a bag of chips on the way home, so I couldn't have been that hungry. The cake was eaten by someone with a large appetite. I'm looking at you Lisa.

A. Discussion

1. Have you ever been in a situation with family or friends where you disagreed over what exactly happened?
   - What was the disagreement about?
   - How did you solve the problem?

2. What does each family member claim to have been doing during the time the crime took place?
   - Given this new information do think any of them are more suspicious than others?

B. Writing

As a friend, write a response to Susan of five to six sentences telling her who you think might have committed the crime and what their motives might have been.

Unit 6 A Day in the Life | 111

07 It Takes All Kinds

Personalities and Habits

WARM UP

Objectives:
- Describe a range of characteristics
- Understand a conversation between siblings about dating
- Describe people and situations in positive or negative ways

PART 1

With a partner, try to match the adjective with its opposite.

- Cheerful
- Shocked
- Worried
- Nervous
- Disappointed

- Satisfied
- Relieved
- Unimpressed
- Depressed
- Relaxed

PART 2 • Discuss the following:

What emotions or personality traits come to mind when you look at each color of the rainbow? Why?

IDIOMS

- **wouldn't hurt a fly**
- **a down-to-earth person**
  He's a very realistic, *down-to-earth guy* who is so gentle he *wouldn't hurt a fly*.
- **wallflower**
- **social butterfly**
  My sister is really shy. She's such a *wall flower*. I'm more of a *social butterfly*.

TONGUE TWISTER

Whether the weather be fine
or whether the weather be not.
Whether the weather be cold
or whether the weather be hot.
We'll weather the weather
whether we like it or not.

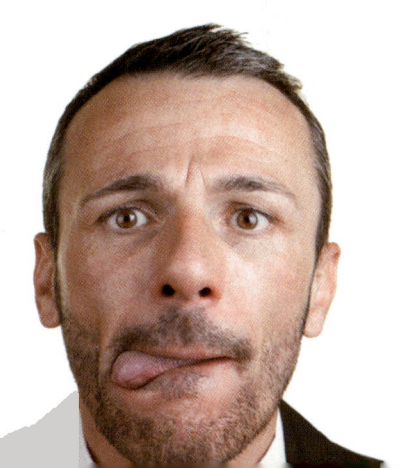

Unit 7 It Takes All Kinds | 113

LESSON 1

A. Shades of Meanings

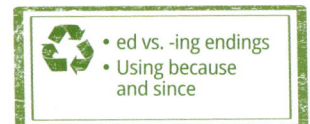
- ed vs. -ing endings
- Using because and since

Language Point: Describing a Range of Emotions

There are a variety of ways to describe different levels of the same emotion.

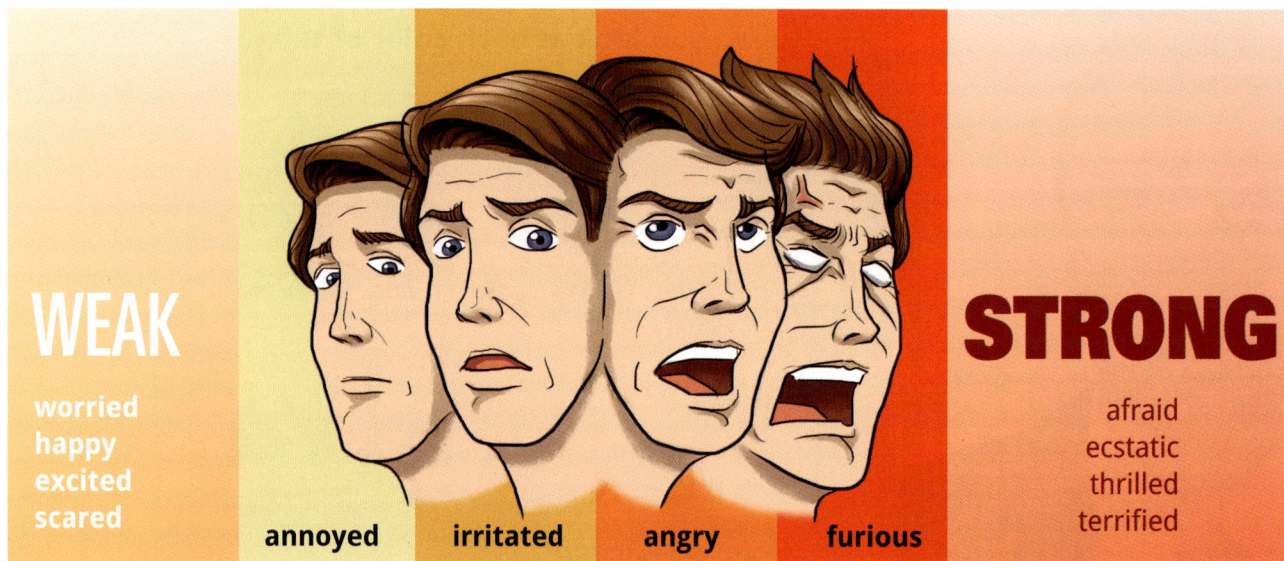

Look at the following situations and discuss how you think each person feels. How would you feel in the same situation?

> **Example:**
>
> **A:** *I think he feels irritated because the man talking on the phone won't get out of his way. How would it make you feel?*
>
> **B:** *I would be furious! I hate it when people are standing in my way and not paying attention.*

a. Tonight, Timmy has a date with a girl he has liked for months. He wants to get a haircut before the big date, but nobody is available to cut his hair today. His sister offers to cut his hair. While she is cutting it, Timmy suddenly hears her say, "Oops." He now has a large bald spot on the middle of his head!

b. Timmy wears a hat on his date, and she doesn't seem to notice there is anything wrong with his hair. On the street, the wind blows his hat off! His date looks at his hair and says, "Wow, your haircut is so modern! I love it!" She gives him a kiss on the cheek.

a. It's Jill's birthday, and nobody says anything to her all day about it. She thinks they all forgot, but she doesn't want to **bring it up.**

b. Jill arrives home and notices all of the lights are off. Her family must have gone out without her. She begins crying as she opens the door. When she turns on the lights, all of her friends and family have thrown a huge surprise party for her.

a. Patrick and Sarah are walking by an old house late at night. Suddenly, Sarah sees a ghost! She runs away screaming. Patrick doesn't move a muscle and holds perfectly still.

b. A television show host comes out of the house. They were filming a reality television show. For not running away, Patrick wins $500. Sarah, on the other hand, wins nothing.

bring up *(phrasal v.)*: to make someone aware of something

B. You Don't Know Jack

Pre-listening

- Do you think people lie about themselves on the Internet? Why or why not?
- Have you ever taken a personality quiz on the Internet or in a magazine?

PART 1 ●

Look at the following pictures of Jack's lifestyle. Discuss what you think they show about Jack's personality.

> **Example:**
>
> **A:** *Jack is sleeping in the library so maybe he's lazy.*
>
> **B:** *But he is AT the library. So maybe he's studious…or at least TRYING to be studious.*

Listening TRACK 14-15

Listen to Jack and Lisa as he takes a dating website quiz. Mark the number that relates to his answer.

Post-listening

PART 1
Now YOU take the quiz. Take turns asking and answering the quiz questions. Explain your answer and ask follow up questions.

PART 2
Compare Jack's feelings about himself with your own.

- What do Jack's answers say about his personality?
- Do you know anyone who is similar to Jack?
- How would you compare yourself to Jack?

Question	1		2		3		4		5	
	Jack	You	Jack	You	Jack	You	Jack	You	Jack	You
Do you consider yourself different from "regular" guys?										
Do you like to help others?										
Do you get stressed a lot?										
Do you like adventure?										
Do you feel education is important?										
Do you consider yourself attractive?										
Do you get along with others well?										

1 = Not at all   3 = Somewhat   5 = Very much

Unit 7 It Takes All Kinds | 117

C. See It My Way

Language Point : Positive vs. Negative Description

There are both positive and negative ways to describe someone or something.

Negative ←——————————————————————————————→ **Positive**

| weird | strange | different | unique |

> **Example:**
> **A:** *My friend has tattoos, and she dyed her hair pink.*
> **B:** *Oh, she sounds really **weird!***
> **A:** *I think her fashion style is **unique**, but I don't think she's **weird.***

Use a positive and a negative adjective to describe each passage.

> **Example:** Gina went to see an independent film with someone.
> **Positive:** *I think Gina enjoyed going to a really **interesting** indie film with her close friend.*
> **Negative:** *I think Gina agreed to go see a **strange** movie with a stranger.*

1 John doesn't weigh very much. He has brown hair, green eyes, and a large nose. He wears casual clothing. *How would you...*
- Describe John's physical features?
- Describe his fashion taste?

2 Nickie collects coins as a hobby. Some of the coins are very old or were hard to find. *How would you...*
- Describe Nickie's hobby?
- Describe her coin collection?

3 A child used a marker to draw an animal on the wall of the living room. *How would you...*
- Describe the child's drawing?
- Describe his parents feeling when they see it?

4 David took Nancy to a new restaurant. They had a salad for an appetizer. Next, they ate meat and vegetables for the main course. They finished the meal with dessert and a drink. *How would you...*
- Describe the restaurant and the meal David and Nancy ate at the restaurant?
- Describe how David and Nancy felt after their dining experience?

5 Kurt enjoys several activities, including bungee jumping, skydiving, and rock climbing. *How would you...*
- Describe Kurt's personality?
- Describe his feeling while doing these activities?

Discussion Questions

1 How **accurately** can you judge a person's personality by your first impression of them?
   ▶ Why do you think so?

2 Do you think it is possible for people to change their personality?
   ▶ Have you ever tried to change something about your personality? Why?

3 Of all the people you have met, whose personality do you admire the most?
   ▶ What do you admire most about that person?

4 Do you think that having certain personality traits can help you be more successful in life?
   ▶ Which characteristics are most important?

5 Do you think a couple with similar personalities is a good match?
   ▶ What benefit might similar personalities have?
   ▶ What disadvantage might it have?

6 How do you usually **deal with** difficult people?
   ▶ Do you forgive their bad behavior, or do you get angry with them?

7 If you could change one part of your personality or character, what would you change? Why?

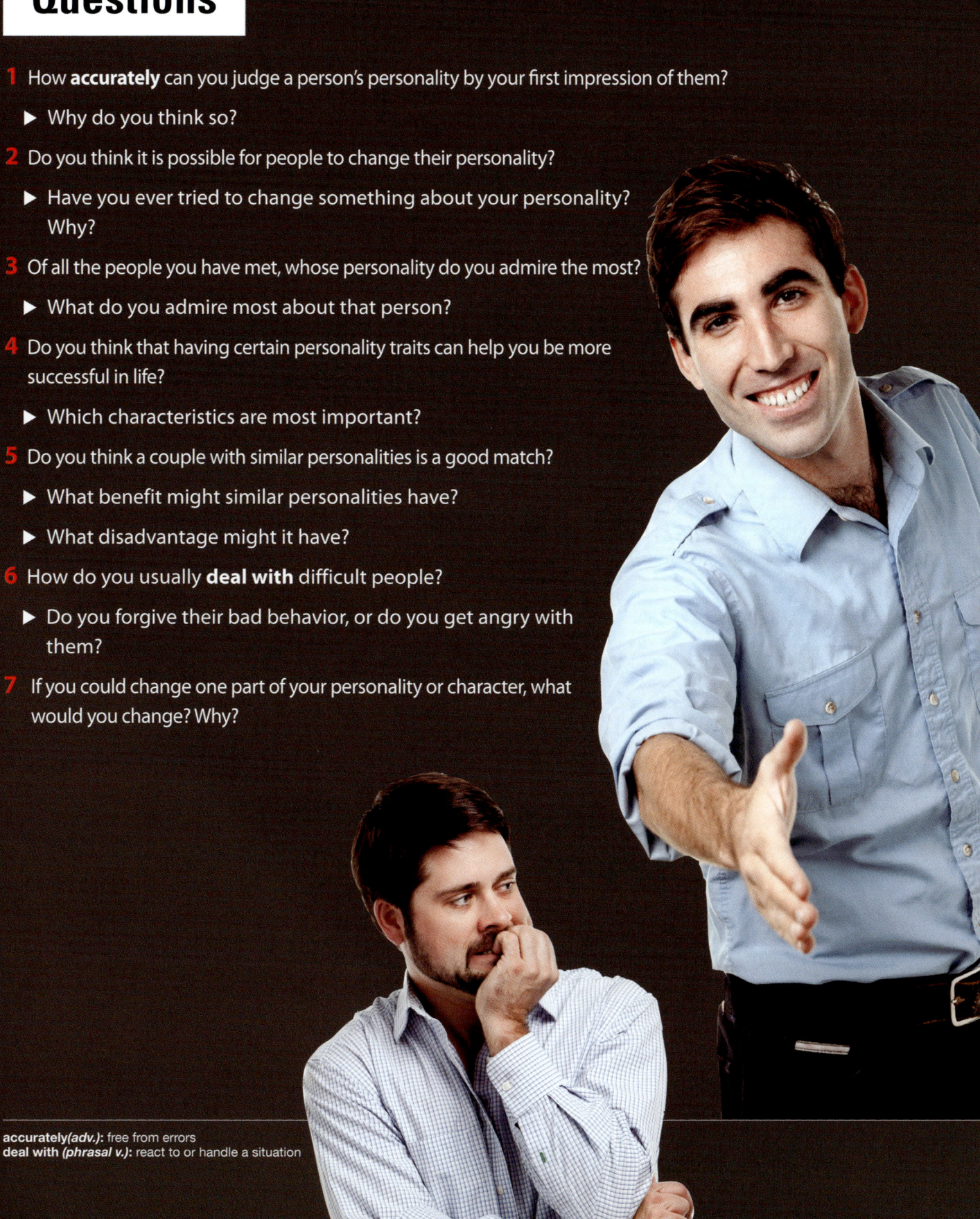

accurately *(adv.)*: free from errors
deal with *(phrasal v.)*: react to or handle a situation

LESSON 2

>> WARM UP

Objectives:
/ Describe ongoing actions that began in the past
/ Describe bad habits
/ Review present perfect

Look at the photos below and discuss the following:
> How would you describe these people's personalities? Why?
> Do you think first impressions are usually correct? Why or why not?

Do You Remember?
- Personality type
- Wouldn't hurt a fly
- Down to earth

A. I've Been Watching You

Lisa and Biff had a wonderful relationship, but recently they have been arguing. What problems do you think they have been having?

Language Point: Describing Ongoing Actions That Began in the Past

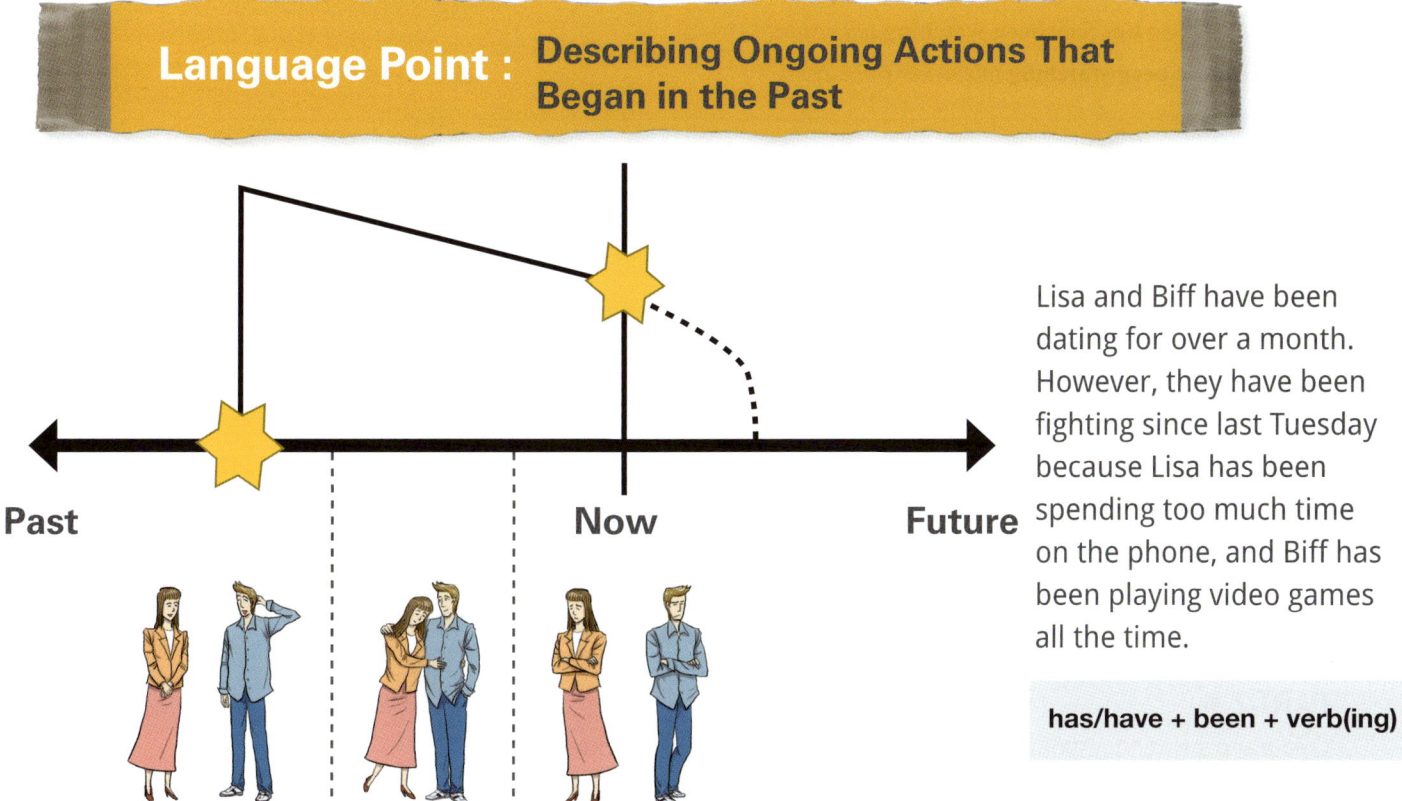

Lisa and Biff have been dating for over a month. However, they have been fighting since last Tuesday because Lisa has been spending too much time on the phone, and Biff has been playing video games all the time.

`has/have + been + verb(ing)`

We can express activities in progress that could continue into the future.

> **Example:**
> They **have been going** out to the movies a lot.
> They **haven't been watching** much television recently.

The present perfect progressive can also be used to emphasize the **duration** of an activity that began in the past using words like: all day, all morning, for, since.

The word for is used to talk about how long the action has been taking place.

> **Example:**
> They have been arguing **for** thirty minutes.

The word since is used to talk about when the action started.

> **Example:**
> It has been going on **since** 2 PM.

PART 1

Make questions and answers about the ongoing actions below. Use for and since to emphasize time in your answer.

> **Example:**
>
> Sam / television / 2pm
>
> **A:** *How long* **has** *Sam* **been watching** *television?*
>
> **B:** *He* **has been watching** *television since 2pm.*

1. Bill / play / baseball / five years
2. Janet / talk / to her boyfriend / three hours
3. Mandy / work / at a café / she started university
4. My mother / yell / at me / this morning
5. Josh / live / in Berlin / June
6. My computer / not work / Tuesday
7. The kids / learn / Taekwondo / middle school
8. Mr. Garcia / not teach / Spanish / three years
9. The students / study / for a math test / Friday
10. The dog / chase / the cat / ten minutes

PART 2

Create and answer questions using the phrases below. Ask follow up questions.

> **Example:**
>
> …..since (a year).
>
> **A:** *What* **have** *you* **been doing** *since 2011?*
>
> **B:** *I've been playing* *ukulele.*
>
> **A:** *Really? What on earth is an ukulele?*

What have you been doing…….

1. since (*day of the week*)?
2. for the last ten minutes?
3. for a long time?
4. recently?
5. since graduating?
6. lately?
7. since (*a year*)?
8. for the last (*a number of hours*)?

B. Bad Habits

Imagine you have the bad habits below. Ask for and give others advice on how to quit the habit.

Example:
A: *I've been picking my nose recently.*
B: *That's terrible! You could try putting some nose plugs up it.*

- Nose picking
- Over spending
- Nail biting
- Smoking
- Drinking
- Playing video games
- Eating fast food
- Drinking coffee

C. Good Job, Stella!

PART 1

Stella is trying to become a better person. Match the negative personality trait on the left with its opposite, positive trait on the right.

1 shy	smart	6 arrogant	polite
2 lazy	generous	7 mean	humble
3 stupid	outgoing	8 unlucky	honest
4 cowardly	brave	9 dishonest	lucky
5 selfish	hard-working	10 rude	kind

PART 2

A. Think of at least two different ways in which Stella has been improving herself lately. Use the present perfect progressive and the words in part 1.

Example:

A: *Stella used to be **shy**. How did she become **more outgoing**?*
B: *She **has been attending** parties. She also **has been reading** books about confidence.*
C: *I also heard that she **has been looking** for a new job.*

B. Ask your partner(s) which adjectives from the box describe him or her best, and give advice on how they could improve themselves.

Example:

A: *Do you think you are more shy or outgoing?*
B: *I feel really shy when meeting new people. What should I do?*
A: *You could try and imagine everyone you meet is wearing a clown nose.*

Discussion Questions

1. What has been worrying you lately?
   ▶ Are you usually a worrier? Why or why not?
2. What kind of bad habits have you had in the past?
   ▶ How did you **overcome** them?
3. What activities have you been doing lately?
   ▶ How can having a hobby improve a person's health?
4. Have you been saving money recently?
   ▶ What do you think is the best way to save money?
5. What are some good habits that you have been trying to get into?
   ▶ Why do you think these habits are important?
6. Do you think your blood type determines your personality?
   How about your **zodiac sign**? (Chinese: Snake, Dragon, Rat; or Western: Gemini, Libra, Scorpio)
7. How do you deal with angry, **bossy**, lazy, or unfriendly people?
8. What kinds of behaviour really annoy you?
   ▶ Why does this behavior annoy you?

UNIT 7 REVIEW

How well can you use:
- ☐ Positive vs. negative ways to describe people or situations?
- ☐ Present progressive to talk about actions that began in the past and continue now?

What do you need to study more?

overcome *(v.):* to deal with a difficult situation
zodiac sign *(n.):* a set of things assigned to a person based on the time they are born
bossy *(adj.):* always giving orders

Activity: Sharp as a Tack

Using similes can be a fun way to describe someone through comparisons. You can make a comparison between an adjective and a noun using "as". Here are some examples:

> A person who is thin can be described like this: *"She's as thin as a rail."*
> A person who is silly can be described like this: *"He's as silly as a goose."*

Now choose words from the list below to complete each simile.

Free	High	Hard
Cool	Drunk	Playful
Strong	Good	Red
Blind	Regular	Quiet
Sober	Clever	Old
Busy	Clear	Sick
Fresh	Light	

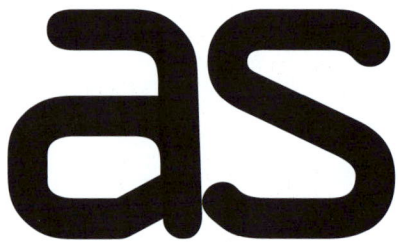

1. A young child is as _____ as a kitten.
2. Shhh! Be as _____ as a mouse! The kids are sleeping!
3. It's as _____ as a feather. I can lift it easily.
4. I always feel as _____ as a daisy after my shower.
5. She's as _____ as a fox. She's very sly.
6. She's as _____ as a beet. She is so embarrassed!
7. My bed is as _____ as a rock. I can't sleep on it.
8. John's as _____ as an ox. He can lift anything.
9. Dave's as _____ as clockwork. He's never late for anything.
10. Mary's as _____ as a bee. She works a lot.
11. Jean's as _____ as the hills. She's 97 now!
12. It's as _____ as a bell. I can hear it very well.
13. Joe's as _____ as a skunk. He drank way too much tonight.
14. He's as _____ as a dog. I hope he feels better soon.
15. Lee is as _____ as a bird. He got out of jail yesterday.
16. He's as _____ as a bat. He needs very thick glasses.
17. The kids were as _____ as gold. I loved babysitting them.
18. Mick's as _____ as a kite. He got some really good news.
19. He's as _____ as a cucumber. He never gets stressed out.
20. He's as _____ as a judge. He never drinks beer with the rest of us.

126 | SLE Generations 2A

LastDitchDating.com

Check your potential date's sign with our Chinese Zodiac compatibility page

The Rat has personality traits such as wit, imagination, and curiosity. Rats have sharp observation skills and are able to understand other people and situations very well. They are full of energy, talkative, and charming. Rats are often seen as being too aggressive and careless.

The Ox has personality traits such as dependability, strength, and determination. Oxen believe that success involves hard work and careful behavior; they don't believe in taking the easy way. Oxen can be judgmental, thinking those who don't work hard are not worthy of their respect.

The Tiger has personality traits such as bravery and competitiveness. Tigers love to be challenged. They don't worry about what will happen because they have a lot of confidence and get others to follow. But don't let their calm appearance fool you; Tigers can be very quick-tempered.

The Rabbit has personality traits such as creativity, compassion, and sensitivity. Rabbits are friendly, outgoing, and prefer the company of others. They also prefer to avoid conflict and approach trouble calmly. Rabbits believe strongly in friends and family and not having strong relationships makes them depressed.

The Dragon has personality traits such as power and ambition. Dragons prefer to live by their own rules and if left alone are usually successful. They're driven and willing to take risks. They're passionate in all they do. This passion can leave them feeling exhausted and unfulfilled.

The Snake has personality traits such as intelligence and gracefulness. When it comes to decision-making, Snakes think very carefully and don't jump into situations. They are effective at getting what they want. But to others this makes them look as if they are scheming and plotting.

The Horse has personality traits such as strength, energy, and an outgoing nature. Extremely animated, Horses thrive when they're the center of attention. Horses love a good time and keep everyone happy with their humor and their wit. But they are often seen as not being serious.

The Ram has personality traits such as dependability and calmness. Rams enjoy being part of a group but prefer the sidelines rather than the center. They like thinking deeply and care about others. Their nurturing personality makes them excellent parents. People find them too reserved and shy.

The Monkey has personality traits such as curiosity and cleverness. They are interested in new things and at figuring out puzzles. Forever playful, Monkeys are the masters of practical jokes. Even though their intentions are always good, the monkey's jokes have a tendency to create hurt feelings.

The Rooster has personality traits such as confidence and motivation. They are skilled at achieving their goals. They are loyal and trustworthy individuals who are blunt when it comes to offering their opinions. Roosters consider themselves very honest; however, their bluntness can seem arrogant and mean to others.

The Dog has personality traits such as loyalty, compatibility, and kindness. They frequently offer kind words and useful advice. Ensuring others happiness is more important than their own wealth or success. Dogs can't help becoming deeply involved in others' lives and are sometimes perceived as nosey.

The Pig has personality traits such as diligence and generosity. Pigs enjoy life and because they are entertaining, others enjoy their company. Pigs are honest and expect to receive honesty in return. They enjoy helping others but can get upset when the favor is not returned.

A. Discussion
1. What's your sign in the Chinese zodiac?
   - Do you think you have any of the positive characteristics in your sign?
   - How about the negative ones?
2. What sign's personality traits do you like the most in a person who you would like to be friends with or date?
3. If you were starting a new business, which sign would you want to start a business with?
   - How about go on a trip?
   - Be stranded on a desert island?

B. Writing
Jack has been trying to find a good match for some time. Based on what you know about Jack, write him an email describing what kind of girl you think would be good for him and why.

08
Good Times

Holidays and Celebrations

Objectives:
- Talk about reasons to get married or get divorced
- Understand and talk about a conversation on marriage
- Give and support opinions during a conversation
- Talk about first impressions

WARM UP

What do you think these people are celebrating?

What are the most important celebrations in a person's life?

COLLOCATIONS

- go out
- throw a party
  I don't really feel like *going out* tonight, let's *throw a party* instead.
- special occasion
- family gathering
  Grandpa's 80th birthday is a very *special occasion,* so we're having a large *family gathering* to celebrate.

IDIOMS

- in full swing
- have a ball
  The party is *in full swing*. Everyone here seems to be *having a ball*.
- life of the party
- bride to be
  In college the *bride to be* was known as the *life of the party*. I hope her husband will be able to keep up!

TONGUE - TWISTER

You've no need to light a night-light
On a light night like tonight,
For a night-light's light's a slight light,
And tonight's a night that's light.
When a night's light, like tonight's light,
It is really not quite right
To light night-lights with their slight lights
On a light night like tonight.

LESSON 1

A. Happily Never After

- expressing opinions
- because and since

PART 1

Read through the list and discuss if you think these are good or bad reasons to get married. Give examples and ask follow-up questions.

> **A:** *Do you think saving money is a good reason for getting married?*
> **B:** *Absolutely. Two people make a great financial team. What do you think?*
> **C:** *That's a terrible reason because money isn't the most important thing in a relationship.*

Some common reasons people get married:

- because of age (getting old)
- to have children
- to avoid being lonely
- to have a lifelong companion
- being in love with each other
- to make parents happy
- to feel like an adult
- because of pregnancy

Do You Know?
- marriage of convenience
- arranged marriage
- common-law marriage
- shotgun wedding
- get married
- be married

PART 2

Read through the list and discuss if you think these are good or bad reasons to get divorced. Give examples, and ask follow-up questions.

Some common reasons people get divorced:

- becoming bored with the relationship
- physical or emotional abuse
- got married too young
- parents or in-laws
- finances
- drug/alcohol addiction
- differences in personal or career goals
- **infidelity**

infidelity (n.): an unfaithful act

130 | SLE Generations 2A

B. Guess Who is Joining the Family

The Thompsons are all guessing what kind of girl their cousin Joe is marrying. Nobody has met her, and the couple hasn't been dating very long.

Pre-listening

Look at the people below, and discuss some of your first impressions. What guesses would you make about them or their personalities based on these pictures?

Listening TRACK 16-17

Now listen and see if you can figure out which of these women is the bride-to-be.

- What does she look like?
- What is her personality like?
- Is there anything interesting about her?

Post-listening

Play a few rounds of 'Guess Who' with the pictures above!

- Start with what her personality may be like.
- Then give some clues about her appearance.

Unit 8 Good Times | 131

C. Celebration Time, Come on!

- expressing opinions
- reasons using because and since

Take on the role of one of the people at a wedding reception. State your opinion on the various parts of the reception. Give reasons for your opinions, and ask follow-up questions.

Example: Walter and Sera

Walter: *So, this is a great reception. What do you think of the **music**?*

Sera: *It's **terrible**! You can't dance to it. I wish there were faster music. What do you think?*

Walter: *I think the **music** is **pretty good**, actually. It's not the best, but it is good for the occasion.*

Sera: *What about the **bride**? Isn't she beautiful?*

Walter: *She's **okay**…*

Sera: *Just **okay**? Are you serious?*

Candy
Wedding: B+
Food: A
Bride: A
Groom: B-
Music: A

Todd
Wedding: C
Food: C
Bride: D
Groom: B
Music: C

McCoy
Wedding: C-
Food: D
Bride: B+
Groom: D
Music: A+

Walter
Wedding: B+
Food: A
Bride: C
Groom: A
Music: B

Sera
Wedding: B-
Food: B+
Bride: A
Groom: C
Music: D

A: best/amazing/etc.   **B:** good/great/etc.   **C:** okay/ not bad/etc.   **D:** bad/ terrible/etc.

---

wedding reception *(n.)*: an event held after a ceremony to celebrate

Discussion Questions

1. What are some ways people celebrate weddings?
   ▶ Where and when was the last wedding that you attended?
2. What are some holidays that are unique to your country?
   ▶ How are they celebrated?
3. What are some examples of holidays that are **commercialized**? For example, during the Christmas season, many people spend a lot of money on presents and decorations.
   ▶ What is your opinion of these kinds of holidays?
4. How are the following events celebrated or honored:
   - ▶ Entering University
   - ▶ Birth
   - ▶ Death
   - ▶ Graduation
   - ▶ Anniversary
   - ▶ Retirement
5. There are many reasons why people celebrate holidays (independence, start of a new year). What are some interesting holidays you know of?
   ▶ Why do people celebrate them?
6. Some countries have strange or unusual holidays. Do you know of any?
   ▶ What happens on these days?
7. What is your favorite holiday?
   ▶ What do you like so much about this day?
8. Have you been to any interesting **festivals**?
   ▶ Where was the festival held?
   ▶ What do people do at the festival?

commercialized *(adj.)*: to use only for financial gain
festival *(n.)*: time of celebration

LESSON 2

>> WARM UP

Objectives:
/ Talk about actions occurring at similar times using *after, before, when, as soon as, while*
/ Tell a story based on a set of pictures
/ Talk about special occasions

What are the most important events in a person's life?

> Which of these *milestones* are important to you, and why?

- First birthday
- Graduation
- Getting married
- Buying a house
- Moving away from family
- First day of school
- Getting a car
- Retiring
- Having children

Do You Remember?
- Throw a party
- Have a ball

milestones (n.): important events that mark a change in a person's life

A. All in the Timing

Language Point : Using Time Clauses

One action happens before or after another:
I saved a lot of money *before* I bought a house.
After she comes, we will leave.

One action happens at the same time as another or very soon after another:
We bought a car *when* my wife got a promotion.
When I see him later, I'm going to tell him.

One action happens during another action's progress:
My parents showed up at the restaurant *while* I was on a date with my girlfriend.
While you're driving him to the party, we'll be setting up the decorations.

◇ Note: Do not use future tense with a time word.
Incorrect:
After she will come, we will leave.

Change the time clause below into a question. Answer using your own words. Remember to ask follow-up questions.

Example: ...**before** you turn 50.
A: *What will you do before you turn 50?*
B: *Before I turn 50, I will start my own business.*
C: *Oh really? What kind of company do you want to run?*
B: *I would like to own my own restaurant. How about you?*

1 ...before you get married.
2 ...after you get up in the morning.
3 ...when you want to have fun.
4 ...while you are riding the subway.
5 When you feel sad...
6 After you finish class...
7 When your family gets together for a holiday...
8 ...as soon as you have enough money.
9 ...when you feel like eating good food.
10 When you were in elementary school...

Unit 8 Good Times | 135

B. Family Memories

The Thompson family has found their old Christmas album from ten years ago. The family is having a hard time remembering exactly what happened. Tell the story of what happened on Christmas Day, adding your own details.

Example:
While the kids were sleeping, Grandpa was putting presents under the tree. Everyone unwrapped their presents after the kids woke up.

7:30 — Wake up

8:00 — Eat breakfast

9:00 — Open presents

The Thompson family
Merry Christmas!

9:30 — Exchange gifts

9:30 — Play games

Go skating

Prepare dinner

Watch a movie

Eat dinner

Play a game

Go to bed

C. Create a Holiday

Invent a new holiday for your country or the world. When will it take place? What will it celebrate? How will it be celebrated? Use time clauses to discuss the particular points of the day. When you are finished, present your holiday.

Example:

Holiday Name: *Bacon Day*

Where it will be celebrated: *United States of America*

Why it will be celebrated: *Bacon Day will celebrate bacon as a food and a way of life.*

How it will be celebrated: *While people are celebrating Bacon Day, every meal will be prepared with bacon.*

Morning: *For breakfast, a meal might include bacon (of course) served with eggs (with bacon in them), pancakes (with bacon in them), and toast with bacon on it.*

Afternoon: *After everyone enjoys breakfast, there will be a bacon parade through town. When the parade starts, Professor Bacon (the mascot of Bacon Day) will throw bacon to the people.*

Evening: *Before the day ends, people will exchange a small present…obviously wrapped in bacon.*

Why do you think it is an important holiday?
Bacon symbolizes health, strength, happiness, and bacon.

Holiday Name:	
Location:	
Reason:	
From morning to night:	
Morning	
Afternoon	
Evening	

Why is this an important holiday?

138 | SLE Generations 2A

Discussion **Questions**

1. Have you ever had to plan a party?
   - If so, what was the occasion?
   - How long did it take to plan the party?
2. Do you like to be the **life of the party** or are you a **wallflower**? Why?
3. What was the last celebration or party that you attended?
   - What were you celebrating?
   - Where was it?
   - Did you have to **dress up**?
4. Have you ever had to prepare food for a special occasion?
   - What was on the menu?
   - Did people enjoy what you prepared?
5. Have you attended a party or a celebration in another country?
   - What was it like?
6. What is the most expensive gift you have ever bought?
   - How much did you spend?
7. When people move into a new house or apartment, they throw a **housewarming** party.
   - Have you ever attended a housewarming party?
   - Who was it for and what did you bring as a gift?

UNIT 8 REVIEW

How well can you use:
- ☐ Talking about two actions using *after, before, when, while*?
- ☐ Language about celebrations?

What do you need to study more?

life of the party *(idiom):* someone who loves socializing
wallflower *(idiom):* someone who is shy in social situations
dress up *(phrasal v.):* to wear nice clothes for an occasion
housewarming party *(n.):* a party to celebrate moving into a new house

Activity: The Proposal

How did Joe pop the question? Work with one or more people to fill out the chart below.

1. a number	2. an adjective	3. an adjective	4. the name of a place
5. the name of a place	6. the name of a place	7. a place to keep money	8. an amount of money
9. the name of a store	10. an adjective	11. a color	12. an item of clothing
13. a color	14. an item of clothing	15. a question	16. a question
17. a part of the body	18. an action	19. a period of time	20. a mode of transportation

Now read the following story to your group, inserting the answers as you go.

After just 1) _____ dates with Katka, Joe knew he was in love. He began to think about proposing. He wanted it to be both 2) _____ and 3) _____. First, he needed to choose the place where he would pop the question. He thought about 4) _____ and 5) _____, but finally chose 6) _____.

Of course, he needed a ring. After he looked in his 7) _____, he decided he could afford to spend 8) _____ on the ring. That would be enough money to buy a ring from 9) _____. After a difficult decision, he finally chose a 10) _____ diamond ring that he hoped would impress Katka.

Before going out, he needed to consider carefully what he would wear. After going through his closet, he selected a 11) _____ 12) _____ and 13) _____ 14) _____ (s).

Finally, the future groom had to think about the words he would use. He couldn't decide between asking her, 15) "_____," or 16) "_____." He decided that it would be best to say whatever was in his 17) _____.

Unfortunately, Joe became terribly nervous when the moment arrived. Instead of asking her to marry him, he accidentally asked her to 18) _____. And instead of saying he wanted to spend the rest of his life with her, he said he wanted to spend 19) _____ with her. Luckily the story has a happy ending. After she accepted, they rode off into the sunset in a(n) 20) _____.

SEGUE

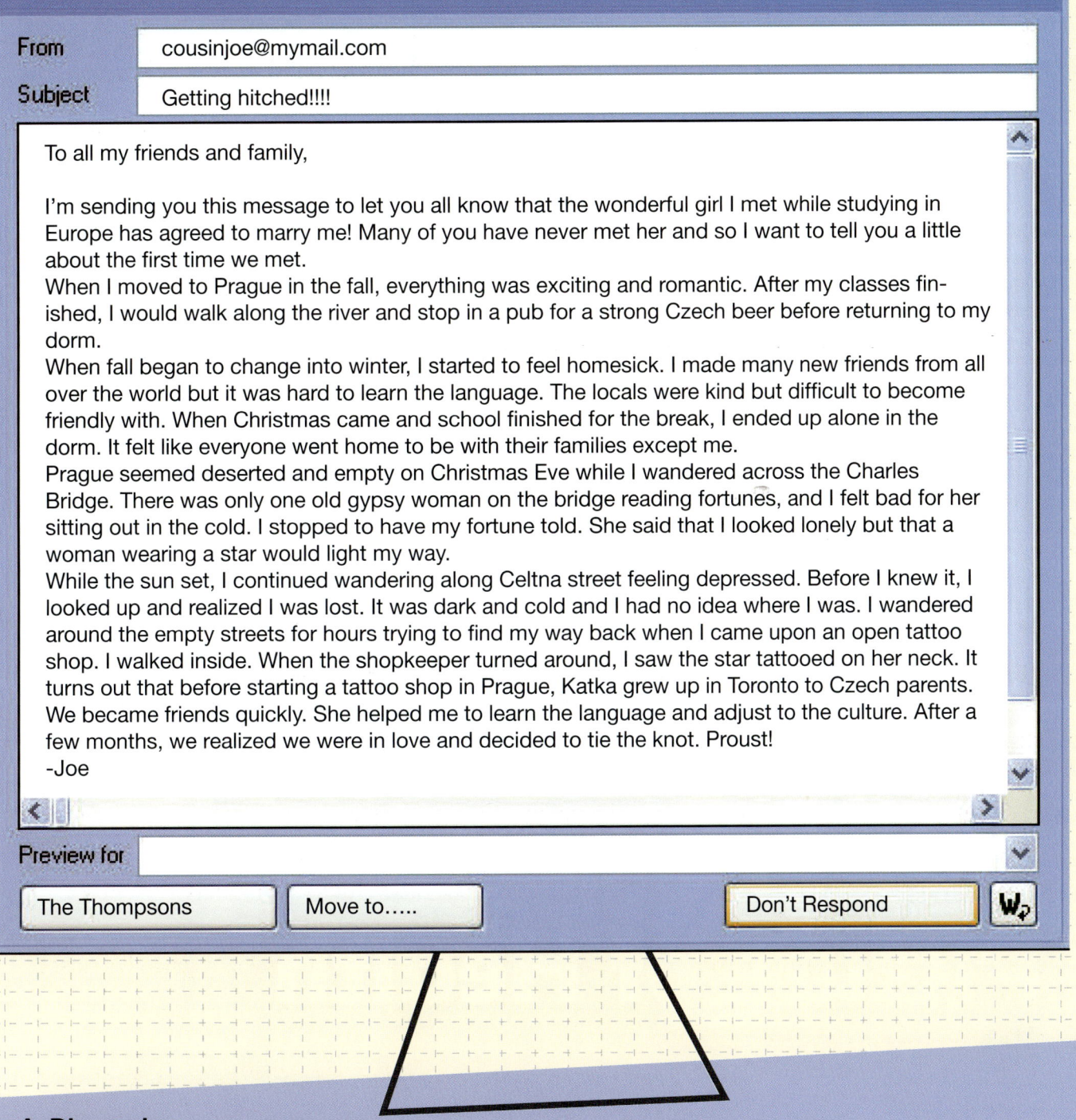

A. Discussion
1. Have you ever moved to a new place or started at a new school where you felt like Joe?
   - What did you do to feel more adjusted?
2. Why might Joe have felt lonely at Christmas time?
   - If you were living overseas, what time of year would make you feel most homesick?
   - What would you miss most?

B. Writing
Write a paragraph detailing a time when you felt alone and how you changed the situation.

09
Picture of Health
Wellbeing

Objectives:
/ Describe health problems using have and feel
/ Listen to a conversation between a husband and his pregnant wife
/ Describe ailments, diagnoses, and treatments

WARM UP

What do you do when you feel under the weather? Look at the photos below, and discuss what you would do in each situation.

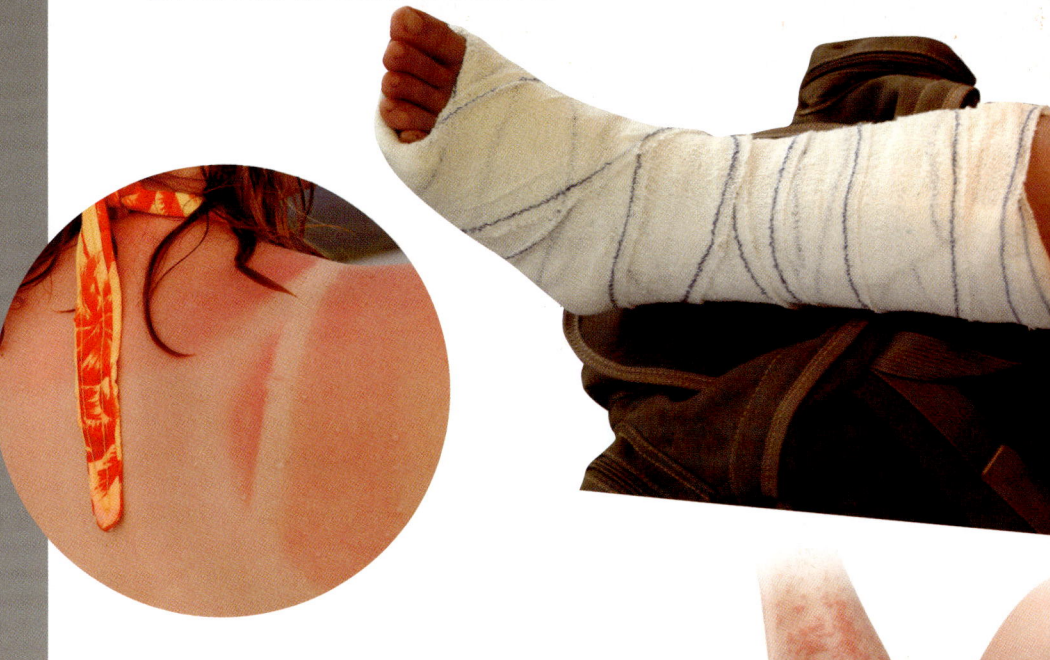

COLLOCATIONS

- **watch what you eat**
- **go on a diet**
  My doctor told me that because I don't *watch what I eat*, I have to *go on a diet*.
- **have an operation**
- **side effect**
  Grandpa *had an operation* on his hip, and one of the *side effects* is a loss of flexibility.

IDIOMS

- **under the weather**
  He's really been feeling *under the weather* lately.
- **hard to swallow**
  The diagnosis the doctor gave me is pretty *hard to swallow*. I'll get a second opinion.

PHRASAL VERBS

- **throw up**
- **come down with (something)**
- **passed out**
  I *threw up* and now I feel like *passing out*.
  I think I'm *coming down with* something.

Unit 9 Picture of Health | 143

LESSON 1

A. How Do You Feel?

Language Point: Describing Health Problems Using *Have* and *Feel*

have
To say what illness or symptom someone has. **have+noun**

Example:
A: *Hey Lola, what's wrong? You don't look so good!*
B: *I have a cold.*

feel
To describe how someone's general condition is. **feel+adjective**

Example:
A: *Hey Lola, what's wrong? You don't look so good!*
B: *I feel awful. I think I'm going to throw up.*

Describe the photos below using have and feel. Why do they feel this way? How did they get sick? When was the last time you felt this way?

Useful Vocabulary

Nouns:	Adjectives:
ache	dizzy
cut	nauseous
the flu	cold
a cold	sick
blister	sore
fever	feverish
rash	stuffy
sore throat	tired

Example:
A: *He feels really tired.*
B: *Why is he so tired?*
A: *Maybe he didn't sleep because he had to study for an exam.*

B. Baby On Board

Pre-listening

Richard and Susan are at home by themselves having dinner. Suddenly, Susan realizes she is about to have her baby! Number the pictures below in a logical order and come up with a story to support your choice.

Listening

 TRACK 18-19

Listen to the dialogue, and see if your order was correct.

Post-listening

What would you do in case of an emergency? What things should you prepare in case of:
- A fire?
- An electricity failure?
- A medical emergency?

How do you prepare for leaving the house before you go:
- To work/school?
- On a trip?
- Out shopping?

Unit 9 Picture of Health | 145

C. What seems to be the problem?

• Asking for and giving advice

Patient:

Symptoms: fever, headache, runny nose, sore throat, cough, sneeze

Symptoms: blood coming out from the nose, pain in and around nose, bruising around nose and eyes

Symptoms: pain, skin discoloration (redness), blisters

Symptoms: stiffness of the spine, discomfort when sitting for long time

Symptoms: stomach pain, burning chest pain

Symptoms: diarrhea, stomach pain, dizzy, dehydrated

Symptoms: irritated skin, pain, redness around a wound, bruising

Grandpa has been feeling under the weather lately. Take turns playing the roles of doctor and patient. Listen to the problem, give a diagnosis, and recommend a treatment.

Example:
Doctor: Come on in. What seems to be the problem?
Patient: Doctor, I have **a pain in my arm**. I think there's something **stuck in the skin**!
Doctor: I think you were **stung by an insect**.
Patient: What should I do?
Doctor: First, I'd better **remove the stinger**. Next, we will **apply some ointment** and I will **prescribe** you some medicine.
Patient: Should I do anything else?
Doctor: Well, you shouldn't **scratch** the area because it could become **infected**. Here's your **prescription**.
Patient: Thank you so much!

Doctor:
Diagnosis: nose bleed
Diagnosis: a cold/the flu
Diagnosis: indigestion/heartburn
Diagnosis: cut or scrape
Diagnosis: sunburn
Diagnosis: back pain
Diagnosis: food poisoning
Diagnosis: other

TREAMENTS

- lean forward/pinch nose
- wash with soap
- rest in bed
- eat more slowly
- take pain killers
- take antacid
- do gentle stretching
- wear a hat and sunscreen
- avoid lifting heavy items
- take antibiotics
- put a bandage on it
- drink lots of fluids
- eat gentle foods

Discussion Questions

1. What do you do in your free time to enjoy yourself?
    - ▶ Do you think these activities help you improve your mental health? Why or why not?
2. Do you suffer from any allergies?
    - ▶ If so, what are the symptoms?
    - ▶ If not, how about your family or friends?
3. What is the most serious injury you have ever had?
    - ▶ How did you treat it?
4. Did you have a cold or the flu last/this winter?
    - ▶ Did you take any medication?
    - ▶ Did the medication have any side effects?
    - ▶ If so, what were they?
5. Do you think you eat a balanced **diet**?
    - ▶ What kind of diet is good for staying healthy?
    - ▶ Why do you think so?
6. What are some **alternative medicines** for common ailments?
    - ▶ Do you think some these remedies are better than doctor prescribed medicine?
7. How often do you go to the doctor?
    - ▶ Do you think your doctor is responsible for keeping you healthy?

diet *(n.)*: the things you eat on a usual basis
alternative medicine *(n.)*: using treatments not considered part of mainstream medicine

LESSON 2

>> WARM UP

Objectives:
/ Talk about ways to relieve stress
/ Use reflexive pronouns

Look at the people in the pictures below, and discuss the questions that follow:

> Which people look healthy? Why do you think so?
> Do you think it is normal to look like this?
> Do you think that you need to lose weight? How much?
> Do you think you need to gain weight? How much?
> Do you think people with a healthy diet are always healthy?

Tip
We do not say, *"I want to lose my weight."*
Instead we say, *"I want to lose weight."*

148 | SLE Generations 2A

A. Keeping Your Cool

- Advice using could/should
- Possibilities using would/could

How stressful are the following situations? What could you do to relieve stress in these situations?

> **A:** *How stressful is going on a blind date?*
> **B:** *It's pretty stressful because I never know what to do or say.*
> **C:** *It would be less stressful if you reminded yourself how the other person feels.*

- Sitting in a traffic jam for two hours
- Going on a blind date
- Moving to another country
- Having your wallet and passport stolen on vacation
- Giving a presentation in English
- Going to a job interview
- Getting fired
- Failing an important exam
- Getting **dumped**
- Getting pregnant before marriage
- **Dealing with** in-laws
- Being diagnosed with a major illness

dumped *(adj.)*: having a relationship terminated hurtfully
deal with *(phrasal v.)*: react to or handle a situation

Unit 9 Picture of Health | 149

B. All by Myself

Language Point : Reflexive Pronouns

Jack looked through the window and saw Mr. Squiggles. Who did Jack see when he looked in the mirror?

> Reflexive pronouns are used when the <u>subject and the object refer to the same person or thing</u>.
> ▶ After he went for a swim, he dried himself off.
>
> Reflexive pronouns are also used <u>to show emphasis</u>.
> ▶ I painted my bedroom myself.
>
> Reflexive pronouns are used to express "alone" or "without company". In this case they are used with the preposition <u>by</u>.
> ▶ They like to spend a lot of time by themselves.

Talk about which of the following you prefer to do alone or with friends and why.

> **Example: shopping**
> **A:** *I like shopping **by myself**. I hate waiting for other people.*
> **B:** *Hmmm. I actually hate shopping **alone**! It is so boring.*
> **C:** *I like clothes shopping **by myself**, but I don't like going to the grocery store alone.*

1. going out at night
2. going to the movies
3. eating at a restaurant
4. working in an office
5. living in a house
6. going for a drive
7. traveling
8. looking at art
9. spending the holidays
10. studying
11. working on a project
12. shopping

C. An Apple a Day

Do the following:
1. Read each profile, and determine if the action is healthy or not.
2. If the action is unhealthy, find a healthier alternative for them using reflexives.

> **Example:**
> **A:** Tasha takes pretty good care of **herself**, but she lives by **herself**. I think she might feel lonely sometimes. That's not healthy.
> **B:** I agree. I feel that she should find a roommate or move in with her parents instead.
> **C:** That might be true, but I would love to live by **myself** because I would feel so free. If she feels lonely, she could get a cat or a dog to keep **herself** company.

Doug
- Exercises alone for two hours a day
- Never cooks for himself (orders delivery instead)
- Works twelve hours a day
- Laughs at himself
- Likes to travel alone

Sandra
- Lives with her parents and seven **siblings**
- Reads books in coffee shops by herself
- Does yoga alone four times a week
- Goes jogging alone at night
- Sings to herself in order to get rid of stress

Philip
- Has three really annoying roommates
- Smokes one pack of cigarettes a day
- Goes drinking alone three times a week
- Spends a lot of time looking at himself in the mirror

Tasha
- Studies alone for 5 hours a day after school
- Does not get enough sleep (five hours a night)
- Goes hiking alone every weekend
- Cooks healthy food for herself every meal
- Lives alone

You
- What healthy things do you do for yourself?
- How about unhealthy habits?
- Do you think that doing certain things by yourself can be healthy? Why or why not?

sibling *(n.)*: brothers and sisters

Discussion Questions

1. Have you ever gone on a diet?
   - If so, what did you eat?
2. Do you prefer to eat out or cook for yourself? Why?
3. What is your favorite fast food restaurant?
   - How often do you eat fast food?
4. Which of the following types of physical activities do you enjoy? Why do you enjoy them?
   - yoga
   - running
   - hiking
   - dancing
   - aerobics
   - swimming
   - riding a bike
   - kickboxing
   - skiing/snowboarding
   - working out
5. Do you exercise regularly?
   - Do you think regular exercise is a good way to prevent health problems?
   - Why do you think so?
6. Do you think children get enough physical exercise these days?
   - Do you think physical education should be required at school?
7. Do you eat **comfort food** when you feel anxious, sad, angry, or bored?
   - If so, what do you eat?
8. What is a good cure for a **hangover**?
   - Why do you think so?

UNIT 9 REVIEW

How well can you use:
- ☐ Describing health problems using have and feel?
- ☐ Reflexive pronouns?

What do you need to study more?

comfort food *(idiom)*: food that makes you feel comfortable
hangover *(n.)*: a terrible feeling after over-consumption of alcohol

Activity: Find Someone Who...Bingo!

Circulate around the class, and write down the name of the person who answers "yes" to any of these questions. Ask some follow-up questions to keep the conversation going.

Example:
A: *Did you get sunburned last summer?*
B: *Yes, I did.*
A: *How did it happen?*
B: *I was at the beach, and I forgot to put on sunscreen.*

Find someone who…

Got sunburned last summer	Has a family member with arthritis	Has had food poisoning	Likes going to the doctor
_____	_____	_____	_____
Wants to be a doctor	Had a headache this week	Has met a nutritionist	Has broken their leg
_____	_____	_____	_____
Has a back problem	Eats a balanced diet	Feels under the weather today	Is allergic to animals
_____	_____	_____	_____
Exercises at least three times a week	Had the flu last winter	Feels stressed out at work or school	Knows a nurse
_____	_____	_____	_____

yourdietbytes.com

SEGUE

PREVIOUS NEXT

▶ Home ▶ Discussions ▶ General ▶ Welcome to Our New Forum

Suz: Hi there, I'm new to the board. I'm a 40-something who just had an unexpected baby. I was much younger when my first two children were born and never had any problems getting the weight off myself. This time around it's proving to be more difficult. I need to lose about 5 kilos. Also, my father-in-law went to the hospital recently claiming that he felt under the weather. He has been diagnosed with high blood pressure and has been told by his doctor that he needs to start taking better care of himself. He needs to lose some weight, probably about 10-12 kilos. We're looking for a diet that is simple and that we could do together for support. Any suggestions?

Bunny F.: Hello! I'm just crazy about the cabbage diet! You have to eat absolutely nothing but cabbages for seven long days and nights. And you'll reduce fat by 5 kilos. Sounds ridiculous, but who cares as long as it works!! There are some side effects from the diet. I tend to feel light-headed, weak, and have suffered from decreased concentration. Wait. What was your question again?

Ima Model: Darling, do yourself a favor and try the cotton ball diet. I just dip cotton wool in strawberry or chocolate food flavoring (0 calories) and binge on that. The cotton balls are very low in calories but very filling, so you're not tempted to eat real food. I'm not a doctor or anything, but I think the cotton balls contain a lot of fiber. It might be hard to swallow but this has helped me to get to a beautiful 40 kilos! And I know it sounds unhealthy, but it's better to eat that and be skinny than to eat something tasty and be fat.

Dr. Acula: Those diets sound ridiculous! What really works is the blood type diet. That's eating food based on your blood type. If you're O type, you eat a high-protein meat diet. If you're A, you eat a vegetarian diet. If you're B, you eat grains and poultry. And if you're AB you eat fish, dairy, and vegetables. It's true because it was designed by a SCIENTIST. Eating this way will not only make you feel better about yourself, but it will also clean your blood.

PREVIOUS NEXT

A. Discussion
1. Do any of these diets sound realistic?
   - What makes the diet sound good or bad?
2. Mom says she needs to lose 5 kilos after having her third baby. Do you think this is good or bad?
   - How about Grandpa being 10 kilos overweight?
3. Have you or anyone you know ever tried a "fad" diet?
   - What did the diet consist of?

B. Writing
Do people care too much about weight in this day and age? What is your opinion of diets and dieting? Write a short paragraph giving your opinion of diets and dieting.

10
Looking Back
Bringing It All Together

Objectives:
- Review language points from previous chapters.
- Evaluate your progress
- Work on communication and decision making skills

WARM UP

LANGUAGE POINTS SELF EVALUATION:

Look at the following list of topics and skills covered throughout the book. Which topics and skills do you feel comfortable using? Which ones could you review?

Unit 1 Social Skills
- ☐ Formal vs. informal greetings
- ☐ Job fields and qualifications

Unit 2 Communication
- ☐ Indirect questions
- ☐ Tag questions

Unit 3 Choices and Consequences
- ☐ Comparatives and superlatives
- ☐ Cause and effect using because and since

Unit 4 Personal and Social Adversity
- ☐ Describing feelings and emotions
- ☐ Advice, suggestions, and demands

Unit 5 Travel and Transportation
- ☐ Expressing likely and unlikely possibilities
- ☐ Making decisions

Unit 6 Routines and Daily Life
- ☐ Active vs. passive voice
- ☐ Causative passive

Unit 7 Personalities and Habits
- ☐ Describing personality
- ☐ Present perfect progressive

Unit 8 Holidays and Celebrations
- ☐ Actions happening around the same time
- ☐ Celebrations

Unit 9 Wellbeing
- ☐ Health problems/symptoms
- ☐ Reflexives

Evaluation

3 = confident using this skill and will use it in the future

2 = need practice but have an overall understanding of the skill

1 = need to work on skill further to feel more confident.

42-54 points: Ready for the next level, 2B

30-42 points: Could move on to 2B but might consider more study in 2A to become accurate

18-30 points: Need further study in 2A to master skills.

LESSON 1

A. The Bemusement Park

PART 1 ● Jack is a new assistant manager at an amusement park. The manager is very lazy and wants Jack to solve all of the park's problems. Help Jack to find solutions for each of the park's problems.

- Suggestions and Demands
- Expressing likely and unlikely possibilities
- Comparatives and superlatives
- Passive voice
- Cause and Effect

Example:

A: *If we don't change the menu, we're going to get sued, and the food's cost is more expensive than taking out a loan.*
B: *I suggest we bring outside food vendors into the park.*
A: *The food should be made with healthy ingredients.*

Problem: The lines at the rides are too long, and customers are getting bored waiting. It also becomes a problem when it is too hot or too cold outside.
Solution:

Problem: The food quality is terrible. Several people have gotten food poisoning. There have been complaints the food is too expensive.
Solution:

Problem: Customers have complained about several rude staff members. Staff members have also been arguing with each other.
Solution:

Problem: Two of the most popular rides keep breaking down. The repairs are expensive.
Solution:

Problem: When the weather is bad, there is nothing to do at the park because the rides have to shut down.
Solution:

Problem: Customer numbers are dropping since a new amusement park opened across town.
Solution:

PART 2 ● Present your ideas to your manager (who looks suspiciously like your teacher). Explain and defend how your idea is better than the ideas of the other assistant managers.

B. Listening

Charles had his health check-up, and Susan asked Lisa to meet him at the hospital. She asked them both to get some ice cream for dessert on their way home. Since it was such a beautiful day, they decided to go through the park!

Pre-listening

- Have you ever gotten lost while trying to find a place? Where were you, and what happened?
- What things do you find distracting while you are trying to concentrate? What are some things that help you to stay focused?

Listening TRACK 20-21

Listen to the dialogue and find out what happened to Charles and Lisa on the way home. Put a number in the circle to order the events as they happened.

Post-listening

In each situation you heard where they went and what happened. Think of two questions to ask a partner.
- A detail about what happened.
- A follow-up question about the location.

Example:

A: *What did Charles and Lisa do after they left the hospital?*
B: *Charles beat Lisa at chess!*
A: *Do you like playing chess?*
B: *I never learned how to play. Do you like it?*

C. Comedy of Errors

Divide into teams. One team should flip a coin to move a square (heads: one space, tails: two spaces). After landing on a space, change the incorrect sentence into a correct sentence or follow the **direction**. A correct answer is worth 3 points. The next team flips the coin to move forward. The team with the most points at the end of the game wins!

START	Most people have eaten rice.	**Say this number:** 1,597	How do you think about that?	After he will come home, we will leave.	The cost is very expensive.
The car repaired yesterday.	Have you playing Tennis all day?	I put on the bus at my home.	I have my teeth check by a dentist.	If it rains, I was wet.	Would you rather to go shopping or to go skating?
Say this number: 13,131	If you want to try a nice restaurant, I demand you go to Pueblos.	He eats too quickly his food.	I have been to Thailand last year.	As a reward for her hard work, Amy was demoted.	He is handsomer than his brother.
Do you got a pen I could borrow?	Tell me about your weekend in Paris?	My teacher talks too much. I am boring.	**Say this number:** 50,005	1. He smokes, doesn't he? 2. Yes, he doesn't.	I have been liking here for years.
Right now, I talk on the phone.	When I was sick, I lost my weight.	I would call if I have a phone	He went to the movie with himself.	This shirt was made by India.	She won't speak to her boyfriend when he will apologize.
Susan is most interesting than Jill.	1. Aren't you tired? 2. No, I'm tired.	What does the **word** mean: The doctor *prescribed* some medicine	**Say this number:** 3,410,217	I have been in Europe last year.	I have been waited in line for three hours. I am so frustrated!
I don't never go to the library.	Do you know she is smart?	He's best singer in the class	My grandfather has died three years ago.	I'll cook dinner while I come home.	I feel flu and have dizzy.
FINISH	You work with sick children? Isn't that flattering?	**Say this number:** 591,006,060	Since we have been working noon to fix the problem.	Could you tell me after class finished?	What does the **word** mean: A *plumber* is coming to fix the sink.

D. We Have a Winner!

PART 1 ● You are judges for an Internet travel site which is giving away a free vacation. Choose who you think most deserves the free vacation. Use comparatives/superlatives, adjectives of emotion, and conditional sentences.

- Adjectives of emotion
- Expressing likely and unlikely possibilities
- Comparatives and superlatives

Example:
A: *I think couple 3 should win because they are **the oldest** and **most interesting**.*
B: *I agree. They deserve an **exciting** time together.*
C: ***If** we **choose** couple 2, they **can take** their kids with them too!*

COUPLE 1

Ages: 29 & 26
From: Australia
Family: No kids
Jobs: Engineer & Marketing Manager
Interests: Photography, Travel, Fitness

COUPLE 2

Ages: 40 & 38
From: France
Family: Three kids (4, 7, 9)
Jobs: Public Servant & Elementary School Teacher
Interests: Fishing, Volunteering, Music

COUPLE 3

Ages: 68 & 65
From: Ireland
Family: Two kids & six grandchildren
Jobs: Retired
Interests: Outdoor Activities, Cooking, Art

COUPLE 4

Ages: 24 & 21
From: Canada
Family: Not yet married
Jobs: High School Teacher & College Student
Interests: Travel, Music, Saving the Environment

Unit 10 Looking Back | 161

PART 2 ● Now choose what they will do during their trip. Select three meals and four activities from the following pages to organize an enjoyable day of fun for them. All prices are per couple. Their budget is $500.

> **Example:**
> **A:** *Hiking is so much fun!* **If** *they did that, they could take so many pictures.*
> **B:** *Hiking is so* **boring**. *Horseback riding is much* **more interesting**.
> **C:** *I agree. Then they* **could** *have lunch at La Traviata. They have* **the best** *food.*

	Breakfast	Lunch	Dinner	Total
Meal Cost				
Location				
Price				
Activity Cost				
Activity				
Price				

Grand Total _____

Activities

Shopping at Super Mall
Transportation Provided

Physical Difficulty ★
Price $20

Hiking Adventure
Local Guide Provided

Physical Difficulty ★★★
Price $80

Horseback Riding
Horses & Local Guide Provided

Physical Difficulty ★★★
Price $100

Spa Universe Resort
Access to all saunas/pools

Physical Difficulty ★
Price $120

Water World Waterpark
Access to all rides/slides

Physical Difficulty ★★
Price $50

Scuba Diving & Snorkeling
Boat & Guide Provided

Physical Difficulty ★★★
Price $150

Helicopter Ride
Pilot Fee Included

Physical Difficulty ★★
Price $200

City Tour Mega Bus
Guide & Transportation Provided

Physical Difficulty ★
Price $45

Art Museum Experience
Tickets & Guide Provided

Physical Difficulty ★
Price $65

E. Review Discussion

Let's discuss what has happened to the Thompson family so far and talk about ourselves. Give reasons for your answers and ask follow up questions.

1 What mistakes has Richard made with his boss?
   ▶ Have you ever embarrassed yourself at work or in school?
2 What qualifications are important for being a manager in a company?

3 Do you remember what **scam** was used to trick poor old Grandma?
   ▶ Do you know if there is anything that we can do to be safer on the Internet?
4 Constantly surfing the Internet is a waste of time, isn't it? Why do you think so?

5 What was the worst thing about Jack's blind date? What would have made it better?
   ▶ Would you prefer going on an exciting date or a relaxing one? Why?
6 Why do you think Internet dating sites have become so popular?

7 How did Lisa feel about everything **on her plate**?
   ▶ How do you feel when you have a lot to do? How do you **cope** with it?
8 What advice would you give to someone who is exhausted? How about bored?

9 Where did the Thompson family go on vacation?
   ▶ Where do you think they will go if they take another family vacation?
10 If you were stuck on a desert island, what three things would you bring with you?

11 What happened to Susan's cake in the kitchen? Who was the cake eaten by?
   ▶ Have you ever had something stolen from you? What happened?
12 What things do you need to have done in the near future? *I need to have my…*

13 What kind of guy does Jack think he is? Would you say he's being honest?
   ▶ How would you describe your personality?
14 What things have you been doing lately to improve your life?

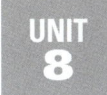
15 What does the woman cousin Joe is marrying look like?
   ▶ Did he make a good decision to get married before his family met her? Why?
16 What would you like to do before you get married? How about after retiring?

17 What symptoms did Susan have before going to the hospital? How did dad feel?
   ▶ What problems did Grandpa have? What should he do to feel better?
18 Do you take good care of yourself? What could you do to be healthier?

19 What predictions can you make about the family in the future?
   ▶ Where will they go? What will they do?
20 What are your plans for studying English? What will you do next?

- Tag questions
- Present perfect continuous
- Reflexive pronouns

Activity: Job Interview

Role-play a job interview with a partner. Ask and answer questions in the following stages of the interview.

Example:

tag question
a So, you're _____, aren't you?
b Yes, I am. It's nice to meet you!

tag question
a Nice to meet you, too. The weather's lovely today, isn't it?
b Yes, it is. I love sunny days!

pres. perf. pro.
a Have you been enjoying the weather recently? What have you been doing?
b Yes, I've been…(details!!)

tag question
a Ok, then. So, just to check, you're here to apply for the _____ position, aren't you?
b Yes, I am.

pres. perf. pro.
a Good - let's start. So, where have you been working?
b I've been working at _____.

reflexives
a Now, I want to ask you: what's something you've achieved by yourself that you feel proud of?
b Well, I _____ by myself. I'm proud of this because…

1 Choose the interviewer and the interviewee and what job you are interviewing for.

2 **Interviewers** use the guidelines to ask your partner questions and follow-up questions.

3 **Interviewees** close your books! Listen carefully to the questions the interviewer asks you, and use the language of the question in your answer.

Interviewer – ask your partner about:
- their identity
- the weather
- why they're here (to check which position/course they're applying for)

Interviewer – ask your partner about:
- recent activities (use some of the following verbs or think of your own):

read	watch	do
play sport	travel	enjoy
think	go	other…

Interviewer – ask your partner about:
- their achievements
- things that they're proud of (e.g., What's something you're proud of achieving?)

LISTENING DIALOGUES SLE 2A

UNIT 1 TRACK 2 and 3

Richard: *(office sounds)* Stupid printer. Hey, you! Can you help me?

Cheryl: Sure, what do you need?

Richard: I'm trying to get this printer to work.

Cheryl: Ah, I see. You have to push the pound key first.

Richard: Great, thanks! I really want to get this report in before five – I don't want to make a bad first impression on the boss.

Cheryl: That's probably a good idea.

Richard: Oh, hey, I'm Richard, by the way. Sorry. I should have introduced myself earlier, but I was in a rush.

Cheryl: It's not a problem. It's a pleasure meeting you, Richard. I'm Cheryl.

Richard: Hi Cheryl. So, how is the boss? I've heard that she is REALLY strict.

Cheryl: Oh, really? Yes, you could say that.

Richard: And that you don't want **to get on her bad side.**

Cheryl: Why not?

Richard: Well, I've heard that she can be a little…impatient.

Cheryl: Mm-hmm.

Richard: And I'd hate to get demoted, or even worse, fired, on my first day of work!

Cheryl: You're right. We wouldn't want that! But I'm sure if you show her you are considerate, hard-working, and organized, you will be just fine. See you later, Richard.

Richard: Thanks for the advice, Cheryl. Have a good day!

Cheryl: You too.

Jim: Hey Rick, what were you talking to Mrs. Stevenson about?

Richard: Mrs. Who?

Jim: Mrs. Stevenson. Our boss?

Richard: Wait…THAT was the boss? Oh no!

UNIT 2 TRACK 4 and 5

Martha: Charles, can you tell me what our **bank account number** is?

Charles: I can't remember what it is. Why do you want to know our bank account number?

Martha: I need to give it to this nice man on the Internet.

Charles: What?

Susan: Mom, what are you talking about? Please tell me who this "nice man" on the Internet is.

Martha: He's a man I saw on television who is trying to save the Egyptian Koalas. So I went to his web page and signed up. Now he sent me an email saying that I need to give him my bank account number.

Susan: Egyptian Koalas?

Martha: Yes, and I want to send him some money to help them.

Charles: Have you heard of koalas in Egypt before?

Martha: Well…no.

Charles: That's because there aren't any.

Martha: I was wondering if there were many koalas in Egypt…

Susan: No, mom, they're from Australia. I don't know who this guy is, but he is lying to you. It's a **scam**.

Martha: But he sounded so nice.

Susan: Sometimes people sound nice so they can **take advantage of** others.

Martha: That is so sad. Oh, well. Now what am I going to do with all of the money I am going to inherit from that wealthy Nigerian billionaire?

Susan: What?

Martha: I don't know how he got my email address, but apparently he wants to send me several million dollars. Such a nice man. I just need to send him $300 first…

Susan: Oh, Mom…

UNIT 3 TRACK 6 and 7

Jack: So. Valerie. Can I call you Val?

Valerie: No. It's Valerie.

Jack: *(Uh)* Okay. Valerie. Are you enjoying dinner?

Valerie: It's not the best. My food needs to be warmer.

Jack: Oh, I can call the waiter.

Valerie: Don't bother. He's an ugly waiter.

Jack: Uh. Okay. Do you like books?

Valerie: No. I hate books. Reading is harder than just watching television.

Jack: I see. Um, so, did you like the new Super Awesome Man movie we saw?

Valerie: I thought it was terrible.

Jack: Really? What was wrong with it?

Valerie: It was too long. And it was slower than the first movie. And less romantic. I hated that movie more than any movie I have ever seen. It was the worst movie ever.

Jack: I'm sorry I asked.

Valerie: This isn't a very popular restaurant, is it?

Jack: I like it.

Valerie: I mean, where are all the pretty people? I am probably the prettiest girl here.

Jack: Excuse me?

Valerie: That girl is uglier than me. The girl over there in the blue dress is uglier than me. *(Ew)*, that girl in the purple skirt is the UGLIEST girl here.

Jack: I…have to leave.

Valerie: Hey, where are you going? You are paying for this meal, aren't you? Jack? Jack? Come back here!!

UNIT 4 TRACK 8 and 9

Lisa: *(ugghhhhh)*

Jack: What is it sis?

Lisa: I'm so frustrated. I told Mary I would go to the movies with her on Thursday night.

Jack: Yeah, so?

Lisa: SO, I have my first Drama Club Session on Thursday night!

Jack: I suggest you let me go to the movies with Mary on Thursday night.

Lisa: *(Eww)*, no.

Susan: Hey guys, what's going on?

Jack: Hey, Mom. Lisa **double-booked** her Thursday night.

Susan: Oh? Well considering she promised to work for me on Thursday night, I hope she can cancel her other plans.

Lisa: Wait. That was THIS Thursday night? I'm so confused.

Susan: And have you finished studying for your maths exam?

Lisa: Not yet, but the exam isn't until…Friday morning. Oh, no!

Jack: Wow, Sis, you have **a lot on your plate.**

Lisa: Mom, what do I do?

Susan: Lisa, I suggest you sort out your **priorities.**

UNIT 5 TRACK 10 and 11

Lisa: So about our family vacation this summer…

Susan: Not this again, Lisa.

Lisa: I know you and Dad want to take a cruise but…

Susan: But what?

Lisa: Well…

Susan: Well?

Lisa: Jack and I really don't want to go on a cruise.

Susan: What? Why not? It will be a lot of fun!

Lisa: More like "a lot of boring."

Susan: Look, I've told you – there's a lot to do on the cruise ship.

Lisa: *(dryly)* You're stuck on a boat for two weeks.

Susan: If we upgrade our tickets, we can take fitness classes –

Lisa: boring.

Susan: Mini-golf –

Lisa: - which is more boring than fitness class.

Susan: Theatre shows –

Lisa: OR we can do something exciting!

Susan: Like what?

Lisa: I want to go skydiving!

Susan: Skydiving? Are you crazy? Can you imagine your father skydiving?

Lisa: Well, Jack thinks we should go camping in the mountains.

Susan: If we go camping, there might be bears! I am terrified of bears!

Lisa: Which is exactly why we should go skydiving.

Susan: *(sigh)* We're going on the cruise.

Lisa: There could be bears on the cruise…

Susan: Oh, hush.

UNIT 6 TRACK *12* and *13*

Susan:

It was a dark night in the cold city. I had finished running errands after a long day of baking a very special strawberry cream cake. I came home around 8pm when I saw it. A terrible crime that had been committed. The cake. The cake I had spent the last two days making had been eaten. There were small pieces of strawberry and icing everywhere. On the table, the chairs, the floor. A single brown hair was found sticking out of the icing. My first clue. I immediately told everyone to come into the kitchen, the scene of the crime.

They all looked nervous.
My loyal husband, Richard; my sweet children, Lisa and Jack; my in-laws Charles and Martha. Nobody trusts their in-laws. And last, but not least, my dear cat, Mr. Squiggles.

The first question I asked them was the most obvious:
Who had been home at the time of the crime. Everybody except Richard and Lisa. Richard was getting his hair cut, he claimed. Lisa had gone to the market.
Lisa also said she didn't like strawberry. My in-laws said they couldn't eat strawberry cake either. But then, nobody trusts their in-laws.
Finally, I walked around the room and noticed some of my "trustworthy" family members had icing on them. Maybe they just stepped in it. Perhaps it was evidence. Icing was on Jack's shoe, and there was more icing on Lisa's jacket. Mr. Squiggles had icing on his foot.
I decided to let them go for now. Jack had forgotten to do his chores, doing the laundry and feeding the cat. Lisa needed to do her homework. Richard went to the bedroom – he said he wasn't feeling well – and my in-laws went to watch TV. Mr. Squiggles stayed with me to think. Who to trust? It was a dark night in the cold city, and out there somewhere, the cake eater was waiting…

UNIT 7 TRACK 14 and 15

Lisa: You really think this dating site is going to help you find a woman?

Jack: Of course. This will tell them why I am the perfect man.

Lisa: Really?

Jack: Let's see. *(Ahh)* Do I consider myself different from regular guys?

Lisa: *(Ha)*, You're like, the weirdest guy I know. Definitely a five.

Jack: Maybe I am a little…unique. How about a four. *(click sound)* Do I like to help others? Of course I do.

Lisa: You never help me.

Jack: Yeah, but you're my sister.

Lisa: Hey!

Jack: Fine. A three.

Lisa: *(clears her throat)*

Jack: Two. *(click sound)* Happy?

Lisa: What's next? Do you get stressed out a lot.

Jack: I'm too organized to get stressed out a lot.

Lisa: You're too lazy to get a job or do any work. So of course you're not stressed out.

Jack: I've TRIED to find a job. But you're right. I have a pretty easy life. So,… one. *(click sound)* Do I like adventure? I am the most adventurous person I know!

Lisa: Are you kidding? You fell asleep when we went hiking in the mountains. That was surprising because you were SO scared that a bear might eat us.

Jack: I was being cautious. At least I went hiking.

Lisa: Three.

Jack: Okay, three. *(click) (Uhh)* Do you feel education is important? Of course. I'm very studious. Five.

Lisa: *(laughing)*

Jack: What?

Lisa: Nothing. It's just that you always fall asleep in the library. And in class. And when you're doing your homework.

Jack: See, I'm ALWAYS working on my studies. Five. *(click)*

Lisa: Oh, jeez. Next. Do you consider yourself attractive? Well. Do you?

Jack: Well, women consider me attractive. And I am the most attractive of my friends.

Lisa: *(laughing)* You're so arrogant!

Jack: No, I'm self-confident. Women like men who are self-confident.

Lisa: Yes, but not men who are too proud.

Jack: So if I choose a lower number, women will like me more?

Lisa: Maybe.

Jack: Okay, two.

Lisa: Not too low. They'll think you're really ugly.

Jack: Three?

Lisa: That's safe. *(click)*

Jack: Last one. Do I get along well with others? Of course. Five. So long as it's not my sister!

Lisa: Hey! *(click)*

UNIT 8 TRACK 16 and 17

Jack: I can't believe Cousin Joe is getting married.

Lisa: I know, and before we've had a chance to meet her.

Jack: I wonder what she's like.

Lisa: She must be pretty special. Do you know anything about her?

Jack: Well, I heard she is really friendly.

Lisa: *(Ah)*, me too. And that she's always smiling.

Jack: Wait a second, is she the girl with the glasses that was at Grandpa's birthday party?

Lisa: No. I don't think she wears glasses.

Jack: And I assume she's blonde, isn't she? He always liked blondes.

Lisa: Actually, no; she's not a blonde.

Jack: Really? Wow.

Lisa: Yeah, she has really dark hair.

Jack: Is she more conservative or liberal?

Lisa: How should I know?

Jack: Well, how long is her hair?

Lisa: I think it's pretty long, but that doesn't mean anything. But..

Jack: But what?

Lisa: I think she has a tattoo.

Jack: Really? Cool. That's pretty liberal.

Lisa: I'm just glad she likes to smile…

Jack: Well, no matter what she is like, I'm sure they'll be very happy together.

UNIT 9 TRACK 18 and 19

Susan: Oh, honey, this pizza is delicious. Is it delivery?

Richard: Actually, no, it's –

Susan: Oh my gosh!

Richard: What? What is it?

Susan: It's the baby! I think the baby is on its way!

Richard: What? Now? But, the pizza! Wait, who cares about the pizza! We're going to have a baby! I haven't packed for the hospital yet…

Susan: Calm down, Richard…

Richard: Where's the suitcase? I already put blankets and food in the suitcase! And my jacket? Where is my jacket? The baby! We're going to have the baby!

Susan: Richard, I am the one who is having the baby, so relax and just…

Richard: I can't believe it's already happening! Do we have gas in the car? What if we don't? We need to hurry!

Susan: Are you even listening to me? ohhh. *(groaning)*

Richard: What if there's traffic? No time to wait!

Susan: Honey, where are you going?

Richard: To the hospital! Oh, and I need to call work…did I pack some extra batteries for the camera?

Susan: Honey?

Richard: Right, that's everything! *(slams door)*

Susan: Honey? *(car sound driving away, then slamming on brakes, car door opening)*

Richard: Oh my gosh, Suz!

Susan: Did you forget somebody?

Richard: I'm so sorry, I was in such a…

Susan: Let's just go. I'll yell at you on the way to the hospital.

UNIT 10 TRACK 20 and 21

Susan: Where have you two been? You should have been back hours ago!

Lisa: Sorry, Mom.

Charles: It was my fault, Susan. After we left the hospital, it was such a beautiful day out – I thought we should go home through the park!

Susan: And that took four hours?

Charles: Well, when we got to the park, we found a place to play chess. I hadn't played in years.

Lisa: But he still beat me.

Charles: It was a close game.

Lisa: Oh, and Mom, after we played chess, we went to the fountain in the center of the park. And there was this boy there!

Charles: Ah, poor boy.

Susan: Why? What was wrong?

Lisa: He couldn't find his mother! They had been bicycling together and he got lost.

Susan: Oh, dear.

Lisa: But we helped him, didn't we, Grandpa?

Charles: We sure did. We found the boy's mother near some apple trees, looking for him! She was so worried!

Lisa: I asked Grandpa if we could stay and eat some apples.

Charles: I can't say no to her.

Lisa: They were so delicious! After, we started to head home…

Charles: I don't think you should tell her this part.

Susan: Why? What happened?

Lisa: We saw a bear!

Susan: A bear!

Lisa: Don't worry, Mom. When we saw the bear, we ran away.

Susan: Dad, you ran?

Lisa: He ran faster than I did!

Charles: I guess I'm not as old as I thought I was.

Susan: Dad!

Lisa: When we got away from the bear, I was so tired!

Charles: I asked her to take a break.

Lisa: So we got some water from a street vendor. We started to go home again, when Grandpa ran into a bunch of his friends! Did you know Grandpa used to be in a jazz band?

Susan: I remember that.

Lisa: Yeah, his friends were in the park playing jazz music! It was amazing!

Charles: I wish I had my trombone with me. It would have been just like old times.

Lisa: Anyway, we listened to them for a little while and then came straight home!

Susan: That is quite a story. I'm just glad you two are safe. So where is the ice cream I asked you to pick up from the market?

Lisa: Oh, Grandpa!

Lisa and Charles: We forgot!

Lisa: Don't worry, Mom. Grandpa and I can go get it!

Susan: Oh, no; you two aren't going anywhere!

GLOSSARY SLE 2A

A

accurately *adverb* free from errors — Unit 7
acquaintance *noun* a person you know who is not a close friend — Unit 1
alternative medicine *noun* treatments not considered part of mainstream medicine — Unit 9

B

backtrack *verb* to return the same way you came — unit 5
beep *verb* to make a short sound as a signal — Unit 2
bland *adjective* having no flavor — Unit 10
blind date *noun* a date in which the two people have never met before — Unit 3
book (something) *verb* to make a reservation for a hotel, restaurant, etc. — Unit 5
bossy *adjective* always giving orders — Unit 7
bring up *phrasal verb* to make someone aware of something — Unit 7
budget *noun* a plan for spending money — Unit 1

C

cannibal *noun* an animal that eats its own kind — Unit 5
chauffeuring *noun* personal driving service — Unit 6
cheat on *idiom* be unfaithful to — Unit 4
comfort food *idiom* food that makes you feel comfortable — Unit 9
commercialized *adjective* used only for financial gain — Unit 8
complaint *noun* a reason for not being satisfied — Unit 1
conservative *adjective* reluctant to accept change (List.)
crack of dawn *idiom* very early in the morning — Unit 6
creativity *noun* the ability to make new things — Unit 1

D

dead end *idiom* a situation with no future — Unit 4
deal with *phrasal verb* react to or handle a situation — Unit 7 and Unit 9
dedication *noun* committed to something — Unit 1
defeat *verb* to win in a competition such as a war or game — Unit 4
degree *noun* a document given to someone who has completed university — Unit 1
demoted *adjective* given a lower position at one's job — Unit 1
diet *noun* the things you eat on a usual basis — Unit 9
disabled *adjective* a physical or mental condition that limits a person's ability — Unit 2
double-book (something) *verb* to have conflicting plans for the same time — Unit 4
dress up *phrasal verb* to wear nice clothes for an occasion — Unit 8
dumped *adjective* having a relationship terminated hurtfully — Unit 9

E

efficient *adjective* able to produce good results without wasting time — Unit 3

engaged *adjective* promised to marry — Unit 1
errand *noun* small job to collect or deliver something — Unit 6

F

festival *noun* time of celebration — Unit 8
fiancée *noun* a woman who is engaged to be married — Unit 4
fired *adjective* dismissed from one's job — Unit 1
first impression *noun* the sense you give someone of yourself upon first meeting — Unit 1
fix up *phrasal verb* to repair or improve — Unit 6
fulfill *verb* satisfy something — Unit 5

G

get on (someone's) bad side *idiom* to have someone dislike you — Unit 1
go along with (something) *idiom* to agree to someone's wants — Unit 3
grade point average (GPA) *noun* a number showing a student's average grade — Unit 1
graduate *noun* a person who has earned a degree — Unit 1
grouchy *adjective* having a bad temper or being in a bad mood — Unit 1
guided tour *noun* a tour that is led by a tour guide — Unit 5

H

handicapped *adjective* having a physical or mental medical condition that limits what someone can do — Unit 1
handle (something) *verb* to deal with a situation — Unit 3
hangover *noun* a terrible feeling after over-consumption of alcohol — Unit 9
hardworking *adjective* using a lot of time and energy to do something — Unit 1
heartbreaking *adjective* making you feel very sad or upset — Unit 4
honesty *noun* truthfulness — Unit 1
horizon *noun* the line where the earth meets the sky — Unit 5
housewarming party *noun* a party to celebrate moving into a new house — Unit 8

I

icing *noun* sugary covering for cake (List.)
imply *verb* to suggest without stating directly — Unit 4
infidelity *noun* an unfaithful act in a relationship — Unit 8
inherit *verb* to receive something when someone dies (List.)
in-laws *noun* related through marriage (List.)
invisible *adjective* unable to be seen — Unit 5

J

job security *noun* the knowledge that an employee will not lose his or her job — Unit 1
judgment *noun* decision making skill — Unit 1

K

L

lay off *phrasal verb* dismissed from one's job due to economic reasons — Unit 1
lavish *adjective* using a large amount of something — Unit 4
layover *noun* a period of time in which one is not traveling between two flights — Unit 5
liberal *adjective* open to change (List.)
life of the party *idiom* someone who loves socializing — Unit 8
look on the bright side *idiom* to see something good in a bad situation — Unit 4

M

make mistakes *verb* to do something wrong — Unit 4
milestones *noun* important events that mark a change in a person's life — Unit 8
mistake *verb* to accidentally think someone is another person — Unit 1
misunderstanding *noun* a mistake made while communicating — Unit 2

N

narrow down *phrasal verb* to limit the amount of things being considered — Unit 6
networking *noun* getting to know other people for employment or business purposes — Unit 2

O

once in a lifetime *idiom* probably not going to happen again — Unit 3
on your plate *idiom* things you have to get done — Unit 4
organization *noun* effective at arrangement — Unit 1
overcome *verb* to deal with a difficult situation — Unit 1 and 7
overwhelmed *adjective* to have too many problems to deal with — Unit 4

P

passion *noun* strong emotions about something — Unit 1
patience *noun* ability to stay calm for a long period of time — Unit 1
pet peeve *noun* something that annoys a person — Unit 3
pick up (someone) *phrasal verb* to collect someone or something from a location — Unit 1
play a trick *idiom* to trick someone into believing something as a joke — Unit 6
play games *idiom* to try and gain advantage by being dishonest — Unit 2
priority *noun* thing of greatest importance — Unit 4
promote *verb* give a higher position at one's job — Unit 1
proof *noun* something that shows that something else is true — Unit 2
prestigious *adjective* having a very good reputation — Unit 1
propose *verb* to make a suggestion — Unit 1
pull (someone) over *idiom* to force someone to move to the side of the road — Unit 4
punctual *adjective* arriving on time — Unit 3

Q

quit *verb* to stop working — Unit 1

R

raining cats and dogs *idiom* raining very hard — Unit 5
raise *noun* a higher salary — Unit 1
raging *adjective* very strong — Unit 5
reference *noun* a person who can give information about someone else's ability. — Unit 1
retire *verb* to end one's job or career because of old age — Unit 1
run late *idiom* not coming at a scheduled time — Unit 6
rush hour *noun* the busiest time for travel before and after work — Unit 5

S

scam *verb* to trick someone into giving money — Unit 2
sibling *noun* brother or sister — Unit 9
sightseeing *noun* visiting places that are interesting when one is on vacation — Unit 5
skeptical *adjective* having doubts about something — Unit 2
skip school *idiom* to not go to school without permission — Unit 1
sleep in *phrasal verb* to sleep late into the day — Unit 6
sober *adjective* not influenced by alcohol — Unit 1
social skill *noun* ability to be friendly — Unit 1
stress out *phrasal verb* to suffer from mental stress — Unit 4
sticking to a schedule *idiom* following a routine closely — Unit 6
sunscreen *noun* lotion that is put on skin to prevent sunburn — Unit 5

T

take advantage of *idiom* to trick someone weaker into something (List.)
take the easy way out *idiom* to free oneself from a difficult situation by avoiding it — Unit 4
tech support *noun* a service that helps customers with a product they have purchased — Unit 2
trustworthy *adjective* someone or something that can be believed — Unit 2

U

undergraduate *noun* a university student who has not earned a degree yet — Unit 1
upcoming *adjective* happening soon — Unit 1

V

W

wallflower *idiom* someone who is shy in social situations — Unit 8
wedding reception *noun* an event held after a ceremony to celebrate — Unit 8
witness *noun* a person who sees an action in progress — Unit 2

X

Y

Z

zodiac sign *noun* a set of things assigned to a person based on the time they are born — Unit 7